GREEK PERSONAL RELIGION
A READER

GREEK PERSONAL RELIGION

A READER

Stephen Instone

Aris and Phillips
is an imprint of
Oxbow Books, Oxford

ISBN 978-0-85668-898-0

A CIP record for this book is available from the British Library

Cover Image: Pythagoras statue, Samos, Greece. Photo by Tim van Woensel
(www.pbase.com/tvw)

Printed in Great Britain by
Hobbs the Printers Ltd, Totton, Hampshire

CONTENTS

Preface   vii

General Introduction   1

Texts, Introductions, Commentaries   8
  1 Homer *Iliad* 1.188–222: A Divine Intervention   8
  2 Hesiod *Works and Days* 724–828: Personal Observance   11
  3 Theophrastus *Characters* 16: Superstition   16
  4 Herodotus 6.105–106: A Divine Epiphany (Pheidippides and Pan) 22
  5 Aeschylus *Agamemnon* 160–183: Hymn to Zeus   26
  6 Pindar *Pythian* Ten: The Victorious Athlete and the Divine   27
  7 Empedocles, selected fragments: The Divine Forces
    of Love and Strife; Metempsychosis and the Divine   33
  8 Plato *Symposium* 209e5–212a7: Divine Forms   45
  9 Aristotle *Nicomachean Ethics* 1177b26–1179a23:
    Divine *theoria*   51
 10 Hippocratic *Sacred Disease* 1–6: Epilepsy   57
 11 *Lex Sacra* from Selinous: Pollution   64
 12, 13 and 14   Orphism   69
 12 Orphism (1): Herodotus 4.78.3–4.80.5, Scyles and Olbia   70
 13 Orphism (2): Gold Leaves, a Selection   73
 14 Orphism (3): The Derveni Papyrus (selected fragments)   77
 15 Curse Tablets   82

Greek Texts   87

Index   119

PREFACE

This book arose from my interest in Pindar and his representation of the victorious athlete as having affinities with the gods. But it was time to move on from Pindar and consider other aspects of Greek life and thought where man has contact with the divine. Divine interventions in Homer grabbed me next and the many ways in which they have been interpreted. All the time, the sudden appearance of Pan to Pheidippides, the proto-marathon-runner, continued to perplex me in my office and encourage me on long runs. So a text-based book focussing on these and other areas where there was human contact with the divine gradually emerged. It being the 21st century, the Greek had to be relegated to the end, but I am most grateful to Clare Litt for allowing it at all. Bob Sharples kindly read through, corrected and commented on a draft of the book. Richard Janko and Simon Hornblower helped me over the choice of passages, and Amanda Cater with proof-reading. But above all I must thank Shelley, Florence and Arthur.

Stephen Instone

While this book was at the printers, my brother Stephen Instone died in Lac Leman, Switzerland. It is at least of some comfort to his family and many friends and colleagues, who will miss him greatly, that before he died he was able to complete it – now his own memorial.

Daniel Instone

GENERAL INTRODUCTION

This is a short book, and so has a short introduction. It is about the ways the Greeks thought gods and individuals interacted and the ways in which individuals could be like gods and have contact with the divine. 'Personal' in the title is intended to make a contrast with civic or polis religion. So this book is not about festivals to the gods, temples, sanctuaries or state-organised cult and rituals. But 'Religion' in the title is less easily hived off. After starting with Homer and Hesiod, the treatment is quite heavily philosophical. This reflects the fact that 'personal religion' is a modern category which in ancient terms falls partly under philosophy. However, the Greek gods permeated other areas of life, so religion inevitably affected also *e.g.* literature, sport, medicine. Poets were inspired by the Muses, an athlete needed the help of a god to excel and an Olympic victor was almost as superhuman as a god, and disease could be seen as physical invasion of one's body by a divine force; the hope by some for personal salvation after death inspired Orphism, a sect popular through much of Greece which helped its members to prepare for meeting the gods of the Underworld; and the powers of the Underworld could be invoked to effect curses on personal enemies. The texts in this book touch on all these activities.

Generally the Greeks believed that the divide between man and god was unbridgeable, and it was hybristic to think otherwise; and in part, human nature was defined by the nature of the immortal gods and their powers, as Apollo tells Diomedes in the *Iliad*: 'Think, son of Tydeus, and withdraw, and do not think yourself equal to the gods, since never will the race of immortal gods and the race of human beings who walk on the ground be the same' (*Iliad* 5.440–2). But there were areas of life where close contact with the divine could be made and was actively encouraged; and the gods themselves could come to one in an epiphany.

More than 30 years ago Walter Burkert, wrote that 'Greek religion, bound to the polis, is public religion to an extreme degree' (*Greek Religion*, English translation by John Raffan (Oxford, 1985), 276); many others have echoed this view. Though Greek religion's roots in the agricultural year and in fertility rites and rituals are still recognised, the emphasis has now turned towards tracing more roots in influences from the East and, as Burkert's statement suggests, the organisation of the polis or city-state. Two massy recent books illustrate the point. *Oxford Readings in Greek Religion* ed. R. Buxton (Oxford, 2007), while having much of interest on polis religion, festivals, sanctuaries, Greek states and oracles, myth and ritual, omits personal religion; *A Companion to Greek Religion* ed. D. Ogden (Oxford, 2007), recognises the personal side, but the chapter on Greek religion and philosophy is about only Plato, and epiphanies feature only as items in the films *Jason and the Argonauts* and *Clash of the Titans*; there is no place in it for superstition, despite Nilsson's remarks nearly 70 years ago: 'The general opinion is that the Greeks of the classical period were happily free from superstition. I am sorry that I am obliged to refute this opinion' (M. P Nilsson, *Greek Popular Religion* (New York, 1940) 111). The smaller *Religion and the Greeks* by R. Garland (London, 1994) gave more space to the personal side, but was not text-based. *Sources for the Study of Greek Religion* edited by D. G. Rice and J. E. Stambaugh (Atlanta, 1979) offers text only and no interpretation. So a book that is both a reader and focuses on the personal side of Greek religion has a place; especially, perhaps, given the recent attention given to one important aspect of personal religion, Orphism, because of the continuing re-interpretation of the Derveni papyrus and new discoveries of Orphic gold leaves.

The book is a reader rather than a sourcebook, so is intended as an interesting and enjoyable introduction to the subject of personal religion rather than a comprehensive work of reference. Inevitably, therefore, many sources and texts relevant to the subject of personal religion have been omitted, *e.g.* oracular responses. This is partly because the number of passages has been kept down so the book can be read through and used as a coursebook, partly because of the need for reasonably substantial texts.

It is natural to start with Homer. The gods' intervention in human affairs happens throughout the *Iliad* and, though somewhat differently, the *Odyssey*. Over the centuries, from the time of the beginnings of Alexandrian scholarship in the 3rd century BC, these interventions have been interpreted in a variety of ways. The passage chosen from the *Iliad* **[Text 1]**, when Athene descends to stop Achilles striking Agamemnon in Bk.1, can be regarded as a literary embellishment of an epiphany. Most Greeks thought the gods were present in the fabric of the world, poets representing them as personifications of superhuman forces or forces outside human control; and sometimes they came to you in an epiphany. But the passage also illustrates a central theme of the *Iliad*, defining man by contrast with the gods: here Achilles' mental fallibility is highlighted, as only with Athene's help can he see the right course of action (not to strike Agamemnon).

For the farmer, heavily dependent on agriculture and factors outside his control such as the weather, the gods were an especially prominent part of everyday life, permeating even trivial daily activities. Hesiod, a contemporary of Homer, composed his *Works and Days* as a poem of practical and moral advice for farmers. The section on superstitions at the end of the poem [**Text 2**] illustrates the extraordinary degree to which the gods could enter the day-to-day-life of Greek working men and women. Some of the precepts seem petty, and scholars used to regard some or all of the section as spurious and not what we would expect from Hesiod. But this view is now generally rejected and the section regarded as providing a valuable and authentic insight into the religious beliefs of archaic Greece. Hesiod *Theogony* 404–452 on the nature and powers of the goddess Hecate is a comparable passage, likewise once believed to be spurious but in fact revealing a great deal about the personal religious beliefs both of Hesiod and his contemporaries.

Theophrastus, though living four centuries later and a philosopher (Aristotle's pupil) illustrates the same subject in one of his humorous Character Sketches. The passage [**Text 3**], besides demonstrating the continuity of ancient Greek superstitious beliefs also provides an example of how interaction with the divine impacted on philosophers as much as anyone else. Though no one doubts the authenticity of the *Characters*, their purpose is much disputed and uncertain. But whatever their purpose, they reveal Theophrastus' interest in human behaviour and the sketch of the Superstitious Man shows the extreme lengths to which superstition could drive one.

The *Iliad* passage was described above as based on an epiphany. Another occurred when during the Persian Wars Pan appeared to Pheidippides while he was running from Athens to get help from Sparta. The story is told by the historian and storyteller Herodotus [**Text 4**]. The Greeks believed gods could appear to runners as much as to heroes; historians accepted the plausibility of such appearances as much as poets did. It is possible to explain away the epiphany as *e.g.* a delusion caused by heat-exhaustion. But there is no evidence Pheidippides was suffering in this way. Underlying it may be the belief that he required the help of a god to accomplish his superhuman feat. Of course, the gods did not always come spontaneously; sometimes you appealed to them for help, often in a short hymn. In the Hymn to Zeus in Aeschylus' *Agamemnon* [**Text 5**] the chorus of old men invoke the most powerful god of all, Zeus, to off-burden their anxiety over the future of the house of Atreus. Another famous example is Sappho's hymn to Aphrodite when she calls upon the goddess to come to her and help her with the torments of a love-affair (Fr. 1). Anyone in any difficulty could call on a god or goddess, and sometimes they helped you and came to you.

The idea suggested above in the case of Pheidippides, that superhuman achievement requires divine assistance and can thereby put one into closer contact with the divine, is especially apparent in Pindar, the fifth-century lyric poet and contemporary of Herodotus and Aeschylus who composed poems for performance in honour of victorious athletes. Pindar both idealises the victorious athlete and warns him to remember his human frailties. Regularly his victory odes contain a mythical section in which it is suggested that by virtue of his superhuman achievement the victorious athlete has an ephemeral quasi-divine status. Sometimes it is hard to see how the myths suggest this, and from antiquity onwards scholars have been puzzled by the relevance of the myths to the rest of the poem. But *Pythian* 10, Pindar's earliest surviving poem **[Text 6]**, makes the points of comparison between the mythical world of gods and heroes and the victor in a clear manner and can be used as a starting-point for analysis of other victory odes.

Empedocles, another contemporary of Pindar, was a poet and philosopher. In the surviving fragments of his work we clearly see both how he integrated the divine into the physical nature of the world and on a personal level his own belief in metempsychosis culminating in his view that he had been reincarnated as a god **[Text 7]**. Because of its fragmentary nature, a holistic interpretation of his work is problematic, but he appears to have integrated his physical and ethical theories by believing that the divine forces of Love and Strife which affect the nature of the physical world through their unending cosmic cycles also affect human nature by enabling a person to change his or her physical nature and to approach, or recede from, the world of the gods.

The idea that it is the philosopher who above all has contact with the divine is stated in a number of his works by Plato with his ideas on Forms, most engagingly in the *Symposium* **[Text 8]**: the philosopher alone has knowledge, and this he has by virtue of his being in contact with divine Forms, objective, unchanging, immortal reality that exists separate from the things in our world, and through this special relationship the philosopher himself acquires their essential characteristics and so becomes quasi-divine. In the *Symposium* this visionary epistemology is expressed in erotic terms, the philosopher's contact with the Forms being in Plato's view the highest form of love; this is because of its context within the *Symposium*, a work about the nature of love, but it is found elsewhere too in Plato's work, in the *Phaedo* and *Republic*. Plato says in the *Symposium* that personal love on a physical level should lead to the impersonal, higher love, and the philosopher's experience is expressed in strongly mystic visual and religious terms, as if knowledge is a kind of religious vision.

Aristotle, Plato's pupil, also thought philosophising was a divine activity, but presents it as an activity any rational human being can perform, not just a philosopher. At the end of his *Nicomachean Ethics* **[Text 9]** he argues that the best activity for human beings is the use of the best part of us, our divine *nous* or intellect, and that by using it we are acting in the most divine way we can as human beings, as well as performing the activity that is happiest and most pleasant. The activity is *theōria* or contemplation, the only activity Aristotle thinks befits the gods, but just what is contemplated is not spelled out by Aristotle: certainly not Platonic Forms, perhaps eternal truths. It is controversial how this activity fits in with the thrust of the rest of *Ethics* which advocates a life of practical virtue as the means to happiness.

On the Sacred Disease describes a range of symptoms generally thought to represent epilepsy, or a disease like it, and rejecting the divine causes commonly alleged by contemporary quacks substitutes a physical cause, a condition of the brain **[Text 10]**. In the course of rejecting the divine cause the anonymous author illustrates how divine intervention was commonly regarded as a cause of disease, saying that Poseidon, Apollo and Hecate were alleged as the causes of certain types of madness. The sort of view the author rejects was widely held: Euripides' *Bacchae* illustrates madness inflicted by Dionysus causing the Bacchants to run wild, Sophocles' *Ajax* shows madness inflicted by Athene causing Ajax' delusion, and in Aeschylus' *Persians* Zeus punishes Xerxes' hybris by sending *ate* into him (just as Agamemnon in the *Iliad* alleges Zeus and *ate* as the cause of the madness that made him foolishly rob Achilles of Briseis). However, such was the hold of conventional religious views that at some points even the author himself accepts them.

The importance of *miasma* or pollution in Greek religious thought was very great: physical impurity tended to imply moral impurity, and both cities and individuals sought strenuously to avoid *miasma*. A fifth-century BC inscription from Selinous in Sicily **[Text 11]** outlines precautions to be taken by both state and individuals against spirits of vengeance. By making contact with, and placating, these higher powers of divine vengeance, the *miasma* can be averted. The context remains unclear so we do not know what prompted the wrath of the avenging spirits – it may have been disease, bloodshed or even infertility. One point of interest that seems to emerge is that when placated the avenging spirits become purer and more divine. Another is the way the inscription appears to blur the distinction between public and private ritual, as it reads like a public proclamation issued by the state for how individuals might choose to act to be rid of the pollution.

The most widespread religious sect in ancient Greece was Orphism. It provided members a release from fear of death and fear of punishment for sins, offering individual salvation and re-birth into a higher form of existence if members correctly carried out prescribed rituals. Just because of its focus on the individual and the personal nature of the initiation practices, much of what went on was usually done in secret, but it overlapped with Pythagorean beliefs and Dionysiac/Bacchic ritual. In the mid-fifth century BC the Scythian king Scyles was put to death for participating in a Greek Orphic/Bacchic cult at Olbia, at the edge of the Greek world on the north coast of the Black Sea. According to Herodotus who tells the story **[Text 12]**, the Scythians did not like the idea of their king being initiated into foreign (Greek) Bacchic rites and raving through the city. The existence of such a cult at Olbia is now confirmed by bone tablets discovered there mentioning Dionysus, Orphics, life, death and the soul, the essential ingredients of Orphic cult. They are similar to, but more simple than, the Orphic gold leaves found in several locations in the Greek world, dating from the late fifth century BC to the second century AD, muddled verse inscriptions on thin leaves of gold that were buried with the deceased to provide instruction about entry to the Underworld to ensure their purification and re-birth **[Text 13]**. The riddling obscurity and poor versification of much of their content mirrors Orphism itself: an obscure mystery cult open to all.

One of the hallmarks of the Orphics was their use of religious texts. Many of the gold leaves are small-scale examples of eschatological poetic narratives. A much longer example of a different sort is the Orphic poem embedded in the Derveni Papyrus, a late-fourth-century BC commentary by an unknown author on Orphic ritual and on a poem attributed to Orpheus. If the author was an Orphic priest himself, this would explain how he had access to the material. He interprets both the rituals and the poem allegorically and through the lens of Presocratic philosophy, aiming to explain Orphism and its literature to initiates by unwrapping its riddles **[Text 14]**. The papyrus, despite huge problems of interpretation because of its incompleteness and our ignorance of the context in which it was written illustrates the hold Orphism had both on ordinary people as a means to release them from fear of death and on 'experts' who could exploit it. It also shows how in ancient Greece philosophy, science and religion overlapped each other.

The religion of 'ordinary people' comes across also in curse tablets [**Text 15**], lead tablets dating from the fifth-century BC onwards, usually deposited in graves, inscribed with instructions for someone, usually a rival in love, trade, the law-courts *etc.*, to be restrained by a supernatural power, often Hermes or another god of the Underworld: invoking supernatural help may have helped people cope with risks and future uncertainty. Sometimes the tablets were deposited along with voodoo dolls, figurines twisted or with nails through them to represent how the curser wanted the victim; sometimes the very shape of the writing imitates the desired outcome.

We have come a long way: from the epiphany of Athene in the *Iliad* to pseudo-scientific interpretation of Orphism, via superstition, epilepsy, athletics victories, life after death, philosophising, pollution and everyday curses. Greeks and the divine interacted in all these areas and others. Greek personal religion permeated Greek life, and went some way towards trying to bridge the gulf between man and god.

TEXTS, INTRODUCTIONS, COMMENTARIES

1. Homer *Iliad* 1.188–222: A Divine Intervention

In this first passage the goddess Athene restrains Achilles, son of Peleus, and dissuades him from striking Agamemnon in retaliation for Agamemnon's announcement that he will take away from Achilles his war-prize Briseis. The gods intervene in human affairs throughout the *Iliad*, and throughout Greek literature and life generally, but this is a particularly striking and dramatic divine intervention, and interpretation of it is controversial. Why is Athene's intervention required in the first place? Why did the poet not say that Achilles restrained himself and himself decided not to strike Agamemnon?

The scene, and others like it in the *Iliad*, are sometimes explained by reference to 'over-determination' whereby what the god causes to happen duplicates what the human being would by himself have caused to happen but additionally makes the human mental activity more concrete and more vivid and helps to explain how a sudden, unexpected or uncanny event could have happened.

However, Athene here does not merely replicate Achilles' decision-making, but provides him with extra reasons for taking a course of action he had not thought of himself: she tells him that if he holds out for requital for the injustice done to him he will be rewarded in triplicate (**22**). Good advice, thinks Achilles, who then comes to realise another, more general, reason for restraining himself: if he does so in obedience to Athene, she in turn will listen to him and help him in the future, for if a person obeys the gods they listen to him, and that is better for him than if they do not (**24–7**). So Athene's intervention provides him with both a particular and a general reason for restraining himself.

But why could not Achilles by himself have provided these extra critical reasons for not striking Agamemnon? Because he is passionately angry. His rage and concentration on immediate revenge have clouded his better judgement and prevent him from seeing what in the long term will be the better course of action and the right thing to do in the circumstances. Athene provides reasons which his rage prevented him from seeing.

The scene is strikingly mirrored at the end of the *Iliad* in Bk. 24.39–140. Here Achilles is again madly raging, and this time is ill-treating and refusing to return Hector's dead body. Zeus, on Apollo's instigation, summons Thetis and tells her to intervene and tell Achilles that what he is doing is wrong and that he will benefit from releasing Hector because Priam will thank him with gifts. Instantly Thetis reports to her son Zeus' mandate. Achilles relents, now that he has been made to see that there are good reasons for doing so, namely because the king of the gods commands it and because he himself can profit from obedience. In both places a sudden divine intervention is required to get him to do the right thing because in his rage he cannot see what that is. Also important are two differences between the two scenes. After Athene's intervention Achilles relents in obedience to her but is still angry and withdraws from battle; but after hearing from Thetis, he calms down and is ready to release Hector's body. And whereas in Bk. 1 Athene has physically to restrain him by pulling his hair (**7**), in the Bk. 24 passage the words of his mother suffice, and later in that Book when he is confronting Priam and contemplating striking him (560–570) he is sufficiently in control of himself to be able to curb himself through his own self-awareness of the will of the gods without the need for an external higher power to intervene. Achilles matures in the course of the poem.

Both passages, especially the one from Bk. 1, show an important way in which the Greeks thought that humans can interact with the gods: humans are relatively weak, are subject to all sorts of outside forces, and for them to be successful in life, whether physically, *e.g.* in war or athletics competition, or mentally in the display of good judgement, they need the help of the most powerful of all outside forces, the gods. A hero such as Achilles, prone to violent passion that can cloud his good judgement, is in particular need of help to assist his judgement.

Bibliography

E. R. Dodds, *The Greeks and the Irrational* (California 1951) 7–14.
B. Williams, *Shame and Necessity* (California 1993) 30.
S. Instone, 'Some Divine Interventions in the *Iliad*', *Eranos* 99 (2002) 103–113.

1. *Il.* 1.188–222
1   Thus he spoke, and grief came over the son of Peleus, and in his shaggy breast his heart debated between two courses of action, whether having drawn his sharp sword from beside his thigh (190) he should break up the assembly and kill Agamemnon, or stop his anger and restrain his temper.
5   While he was debating these things in his mind and heart, and began to

draw his great sword from its sheath, Athene came from heaven. For the goddess white-armed Hera, loving and caring for both equally, had sent her forth (195). She stood behind him, and seized the son of Peleus by his golden hair, appearing to him alone; none of the others could see her.

10   Achilles was amazed, he turned round, he immediately recognised Pallas Athene. Her eyes appeared terrible to him (200), and uttering winged words he spoke to her: 'Why now have you come, child of aegis-bering Zeus? Is it to see the arrogance of Agamemnon son of Atreus? But I shall speak out to you, and I think this shall actually be fulfilled: by

15   his own acts of insolence he could perhaps lose his life (205).'

To him in turn spoke the goddess grey-eyed Athene. 'I have come from heaven to stop your passion, if you'll obey me. For the goddess white-armed Hera, loving and caring for both of you equally, sent me forth. But come, stop your quarrel, and don't draw your sword with your hand

20   (210), but truly you reproach him with words as to how it shall be, come what may. For thus shall I speak out, and this shall actually be fulfilled: one day three times as many glorious gifts shall be present for you because of his arrogance. But you hold back and obey us.'

In reply swift-footed Achilles said to her (215): 'It is necessary,

25   goddess, for one to safeguard the advice of you two, even if one is very enraged in one's heart. For thus is better. Whoever obeys the gods, they very much listen to him.' He spoke and held his heavy hand on the silver handle, and thrust the great sword into its hilt again, nor did he disobey (220) the word of Athene. And she went to Olympus, to the home of aegis-

30   bearing Zeus among the other gods.

1–2 *shaggy breast*: The epithet could indicate that Achilles' animal passions are mounting.

7 *Hera*: the epiphany that follows is presented as if from Hera's eye-view. See also on **25** below.

8–9 Her pulling him by the hair indicates her control over him.

9 Why does she appear to him alone? It is Achilles alone whom Athene wishes to influence, and he would have appeared as a laughing-stock, if she had acted as she did in full view of the rest of the Greeks, and would therefore have been less amenable to her persuasion.

10–11 *Achilles ... Athene*: The staccato three-part sentence imitates Achilles' amazement.

22 *fulfilled*: She makes her idea, that he should relent, acceptable to Achilles, by mimicking in her proposal the very phraseology he had just used to preface his

intention to kill Agamemnon (**14**). The repetition is part of her persuasive rhetoric. **25** *of you two*: Achilles recognises that not just one but two goddesses are working in tandem to dissuade him: he is outnumbered and overpowered. We now see another reason why Hera's involvement was mentioned earlier (**7, 18**).

26–7 *For thus ... listen to him*: It is better for a person to obey the gods, because then they in turn will help him.

2. Hesiod *Works and Days* 724–828: Personal Observance

The primary purpose of Hesiod's *Works and Days* is to outline the agricultural tasks a farmer needs to undertake if he is to avoid idleness and injustice and lead a just and prosperous life. Piety was important for the farmer as the gods controlled so many aspects of the agricultural world: sacrifice to them and pour libations to get them on your side when you are enlarging your estate (336–341), when ploughing and sowing pray to Zeus and Demeter (465). But whereas a prayer to Demeter, goddess of grain, when sowing, is rational, many of the injunctions in the first part (**1–33**) of the passage below from the end of the *Works and Days* are not provided with any rational justification and hence belong to the world of superstitious taboos. This is particularly so in the *Days* section (**33–83**) with its injunctions about which days are favourable and unfavourable for various activities. Throughout much of the first part, however, underlying the injunctions is the need to avoid pollution, to be clean physically on the (often unstated) grounds that physical uncleanliness implies moral and hence religious impurity. In consequence, this section may seem to us more full of superstition than it would have done to Hesiod and his audience.

Bibliography

E. R. Dodds, 'The Religion of the Ordinary Man in Classical Greece', in *The Ancient Concept of Progress and Other Essays* (Oxford 1973), 140–155.

M. L. West (ed.), *Hesiod: Works and Days* (Oxford 1978).

R. Parker, *Miasma* (Oxford 1983), 291–294.

R. Parker, 'Spartan Religion', in *Classical Sparta* ed. A. Powell (London 1989), 142–172.

1   Don't ever at dawn pour to Zeus a libation of sparkling wine with unwashed hands, nor to the other immortals (725). For, you know, they do not listen to you and spit out your prayers. And be mindful not to pee standing up turned facing the sun; and when it is setting and until

5   it is rising, remember, do not urinate on the road nor off the road while
       walking; and not with your clothes off: nights belong to the blessed ones
       (730). But the godlike man does it sitting down, knowing what's wise, or
       having gone up to the wall of a well-fenced courtyard. And don't, when
       you are defiled with semen, expose your genitals inside a house near the
10   hearth, but avoid it. And sow your seed when returning home not from
       an ill-omened funeral (735), but from a banquet for the immortals. And
       do not ever urinate in the mouths of rivers flowing forwards towards
       the sea nor in springs, but keep well away; nor relieve yourself in them,
       for that is not preferable. And don't ever cross on foot the fair-flowing
15   water of immortal rivers, until, looking into their fair streams, you
       pray, having washed your hands in lovely clear water. Whoever crosses
       a river unclean through wickedness or hands (740), with him the gods
       are rightly angry and in the future they give grief.
            And at a cheerful banquet of the gods do not from your hand cut with
20   shining iron the dry from the fresh; nor ever place a wine-pourer above a
       mixing bowl when people are drinking, for a destructive fate is attached
       to it (745). And do not when constructing a house leave it unsmoothed,
       lest a screaming crow should sit on it and caw. And do not eat or wash
       taking from unconsecrated pots, since in them too is a penalty. And don't
25   sit a 12-day-old child on tombs, for it is better not to (750): it makes a
       man unmanly; nor one 12 months old: this too is equally bad. And a man
       should not clean his skin in water a woman has used, since for a time
       there is a grievous penalty attached to this too. And at sacrifices (755)
       don't find fault with what cannot be revealed: god is rightly angry with
30   this too. Act thus, and shun the terrible rumour of men (760). For evil
       rumour is light enough for one to promote it very easily, but troublesome
       to bear and difficult to put aside. And no rumour which many people
       spread completely dies: it too is a god. Carefully and accurately describe
       to your slaves the days that come from Zeus (765). The 30th day of
35   the month is best for overseeing work and distributing rations, provided
       the people are celebrating it having judged it correctly. For the days that
       come from wise Zeus are these: to start with, the first, fourth and seventh
       are holy days (770) (for on the last Leto gave birth to Apollo of the
       golden sword), and the eighth and ninth. Nevertheless, with the moon
40   increasing in size, two days are excellent for labouring over work
       pertaining to humans, the 11th and 12th. Both are good for combing
       sheep and gathering the cheering harvest (775), but the 12th is much

better than the 11th, for on it the high-flying spider spins its webs after midday, and it is when the ant gathers a heap; and on it a woman should
45 set up her loom and get her work ready.

Avoid sowing seed on the 13th of the month that is in progress (780); it is best for tending plants. The middle sixth is very unsuitable for plants, but good for the birth of male children; but it is unsuitable for a girl, either in the first place to be born or to get married. Nor is the
50 first sixth fitting for a girl to be born (785), but for castrating kids and flocks of sheep, and a kind day for putting round a sheep-pen. And it is good for the birth of a male child: but he is likely to enjoy uttering taunts, and lies, and crafty words and secret talk. On the eighth of the month castrate the boar and loud-bellowing ox (790), and on the twelfth
55 hard-working mules. On the great 20th, in the middle of the day, a wise man should be born, for he will be equipped with an excellent mind. The tenth is good for producing a male offspring, and the middle fourth good for a girl; and on it tame, applying your hands, your sheep and shambling curly-horned oxen (795), and saw-toothed dog and hard-
60 working mules. But take care in your heart to avoid vexing your heart with grief on the fourth of both the declining and beginning month, for it is a very special day. On the fourth of the month, bring home a wife (800), having interpreted the bird-omens which are best for this action. But shun the fifths, for they are troublesome and destructive. For they
65 say that on the fifth the Erinyes attended the birth of Horkus, whom Strife bore to be a pain to perjurers.

On the middle eighth scatter Demeter's holy corn (805) on a well-rolled threshing-floor, observing very carefully, and the woodcutter should cut planks for storehouses, and for ships many pieces of wood, the sort
70 suitable for ships. And on the fourth start constructing narrow ships. The middle ninth is a better day during the afternoon (810); the first ninth is a complete bane for people; yet even this is good for man and woman to beget and bear, and not an utterly evil day. Again, few people know that the third ninth of the month is best for starting a wine-jar and putting the
75 yoke on the neck (815) of oxen and mules and swift-footed horses and for dragging your many-bolted fast ship into the wine-dark sea; **65** but few people call it by its true name. On the middle fourth open a jar – it is a holy day above all others. Again, few know that the 21st of the month is best (820) with dawn arising, and it is worse during the afternoon.
80 These days are a great boon for people on earth; the others sound

changeable, neutral, bringing nothing. Different people praise different days, but few have knowledge. At one time one of those days is a stepmother (825), at another a mother. Happy and blessed is he who, knowing all these things, works guiltless in the eyes of the gods, judging
85 birds and shunning transgressions.

1–33 Various injunctions on how to avoid pollution and in consequence offending the gods; the link between the two is that physical uncleanliness implies moral, and hence religious, uncleanliness. On the whole section essential reading is R. Parker, *Miasma*, 291–4.
Hesiod's advice is as follows:

1   Do not pour libations to Zeus with unwashed hands **(1–2)**.
2   Do not urinate facing the sun or at night **(3–6)**.
3   Defecate out of sight **(7–8)**.
4   Avoid sex in the home or near the hearth or after a funeral **(8–11)**.
5   Do not urinate/shit in water **(12–13)**.
6   Do not cross a river until you are pure **(14–18)**
7   Do not cut your nails at a sacrifice **(19–20)**.
8   Do not place a wine-jug above a mixing-bowl while people are drinking **(21)**.
9   Do not leave your house half-built **(22–3)**
10 Do not use a pot unless it has already been used for sacrificial purposes **(23–4)**.
11 Do not put a boy on a tomb or wash in a woman's water, to avoid loss of masculinity **(24–8)**.
12 Use good language at a sacrifice (the danger of ill-spoken words) **(28–30)**.
13 The dangers of ill-spoken words in general **(30–3)**.

The advice involves a mixture of items, some of which are designed to avoid harming the individual, others the environment.
1–2 Because you will be unclean/impure/polluted in the eyes of the gods.
3–5 The purity of the sun, who sees all, will be defiled if it sees an impure act such as urination.
4–6 *and when it is setting ... blessed ones*: if the order of the lines is correct, Hesiod appears to say 'Do not urinate at all during the night between sunset and sunrise as nightime is holy and you will make it impure'. Babies must have been excluded from his injunctions.
5–6 *nor off the road while walking*: as, especially in the dark, some of your urine may end up on the road and pollute it.
6 *and not with your clothes off*: to avoid offending the gods (rather than to avoid being harmed), as the next lines suggest.

7 *the godlike man*: the man who observes this rule is 'knowing what's wise', *i.e.* has a special knowledge bestowed by the gods (cf. **73** 'few people know' how good the 27th (?) of the month is; similarly, on how only a select few understand the rules, **77, 78, 82**. Parker 292: 'The ordinary individual can, it is implied, approach the wisdom of the godlike man by obedience to the rules').

10 Sex causes uncleanliness and impurity, and the hearthfire is especially pure (Parker 76–7).

10–11 Having said where not to have sex, because of the risk of pollution and offence to the gods, Hesiod changes tack and now says when the best time for sex is, after a sacrifice when the gods are happy and least likely to take offence. Upon return from a funeral is a bad time for sex, because contact with death may endanger the reproductive process/virility; cf. **24–6** below, Parker 53).

14–16 *And ... clear water*: further strictures on where not to urinate/defecate. The position of these lines within the passage is uncertain; here they provide a link between urination and rivers. Seawater was regarded as especially purificatory, so defiling it is to be avoided at all costs (cf. **Text 3** below on Theophrastus 16.30, Parker 226–7). For the holiness of rivers and springs and the need to keep them clear of contamination, cf. Parker 293 n.59.

16–18 *Whoever ... grief*: a clear example of the link between physical and religious uncleanliness.

16–24 *Whoever ... penalty*: West points out how here especially in the Greek the precepts form two-line units. This is perhaps so they could be remembered, and hence acted on, more easily.

19–20 *And ... fresh*: because jettisoning waste-products is dirty and polluting.

20–2 *nor ... it:* in case it falls down, smashes the mixing-bowl, and splashes and defiles the drinkers.

22–3 *And ... caw*: 'Roofs are in general a focal point for superstition' (West). Screaming birds are a bad omen (Theophr. *Ch.* 16.17 cj.); one doing so over your head is even worse. Implicit may also be the need to avoid bird-shit and pollution to your home.

23–4 *And ... penalty*: the point behind the recommendation is uncertain, but the idea maybe that a pot used for sacrificing, *i.e.* a consecrated pot, is guaranteed to be pure and sterilised, as nowadays one is recommended to boil water in a new kettle several times before using it for drinking purposes.

24–6 Cf. **11** 'funeral': death pollutes, in particular the sterility of a tomb inflicts sterility on someone in contact with it. It is not clear why Hesiod should single out 12 days and 12 months as particularly dangerous ages; perhaps babies and toddlers are represented.

26–8 *And ... too*: since these lines follow a recommendation to avoid loss of virility, it seems likely that the same point is implicit here too: a woman's water de-mans a man (cf. Parker 103).

28–9 *at sacrifices don't find fault with what cannot be revealed*: meaning unclear. Do not 'carp balefully' (West); perhaps, 'Don't find fault with what cannot be revealed' *i.e.* with religious secrets. In any case, unclean words are unsuitable in the presence of the gods, a theme taken up in the following lines (**30–3**).

30–3 Ill-spoken words are not easily forgotten: avoid their use.

33 Rumour is as powerful as a god – it can easily ruin a man and is not easily put aside. There was an altar (5th/4th century BC) to Rumour at Athens, along with ones to Piety, Shame, Effort (Paus. 1.17.1).

33–83 Favourable and unfavourable days. Hesiod said earlier (303–4, 398) in the *Works and Days* that it was the will of the gods that man must work for a livelihood and that the gods worked out the tasks we must do; Zeus decided what qualities each day of the month has (**34**). So according to Hesiod the impact of the gods on our lives is heavy.

34–6 *The 30th day … correctly*: disputes could arise about which was the last day of the month. Hesiod's point is that the 30th (last day) of the month is the right day to do what he specifies, provided you've got the right day.

47 *The middle sixth*: here and elsewhere in what follows the month is conceived of as divided into three ten-day segments, a system used at Argos; see West p. 350.

49–53 *Nor … talk*: perhaps because the day is associated with Hermes, god of herdsmen, craftiness and eloquence

55 The 20th is 'great' because 'one of the cardinal points of the Greek month; it was here that they usually stopped counting forwards and began counting down again' (West). Knowledge is required to understand the days, and a wise father will produce a wise son; cf. on **73** 'few people' below.

61 *on the fourth of both the declining and beginning month*: the fourth of the second half of the month, *i.e.* the 27th counting back inclusively (see on **55**), and the fourth.

64 *the fifths*: the fifth of each group of ten days, *i.e.* the 5th, 15th, 26th (see on **55**).

65 Both Erinyes, deities of retribution, (cf. *Il*. 19.259–260) and the god Horkus/ Oath (*Works and Days* 219) can punish perjurors.

73 As the poem draws to a close, Hesiod emphasises more and more the need for special knowledge, resulting in a good relationship with the gods (**84**), to grasp the significance of different days. See above on **7**.

83 Stepmothers are proverbially bad or wicked, mothers by contrast good.

82–5 The poem ends on an almost mystical note: if you have the special knowledge required to grasp the meaning of the days, you will be blessed (as were those who knew the secrets of the mysteries).

84–5 For the importance of bird-divination, cf. **64** 'bird-omens'. The line may also have served as a link to Hesiod's poem 'On bird divination'.

3. Theophrastus *Characters* 16: Superstition

Theophrastus (*c*. 371–387 B.C.) was a polymath and Aristotle's successor as head of the Lyceum in Athens. The purpose of the *Characters* is disputed: perhaps they were intended as ready-made material to be used by comic playwrights or orators in their portrayal of types of character in comedies or speeches, or perhaps they were intended as sketches for use in popular, public, entertaining lectures by Theophrastus himself.

The superstitious man is beset by fear of god, misconstruing every little unexpected event as a bad omen that must be averted by purifying himself of pollution. His world down to the smallest detail is beset by divine powers which he cannot avoid and must try to assuage. Although in general tenor and some details (see on **18–21**, **23**) Theophrastus is writing about the same phenomena as Hesiod did in *Works and Days*, there are important differences. Hesiod believes the gods can help as well as harm; Theophrastus' superstitious man believes the gods are intent only on harming him. The superstitious man has a character defect (whereas Hesiod describes what is the right attitude to have); he is cowardly, so that to avert his evil omens he regularly relies on others (a passer-by **6**, a local interpreter **13**, a cobbler **14**, seers **24**, priestesses **32**). The way he is beset by anxiety down to every detail is brought out by the way in which Theophrastus covers every eventuality ('If it's a snake … if it's a poisonous one' **6–8**, 'accompanied by his wife, or if she can't make it by his nurse' **27–8**, 'on seeing a madman or an epileptic …' **32–3**). In addition, some references would be out of place in Hesiod's era, Sabazius **8**, Hermaphroditus **23**.

The superstitious man takes superstition to comical extremes; there was clearly a burdgeoning industry of religious advisers, and he makes maximum use of them. For the superstitious man, large-scale state cult has been replaced in importance by small-scale, local, personal religious practice on the fringes of traditional Greek religion. So, he appeals to the informal, 'new' deity Sabazius (**8**), garlands his own Hermaphrodite statues (**23**), approaches itinerant Orphic priests; he does not act in concert with other members of the community, and is not said to participate in major state cults.

The Greek text is often uncertain; the uncertainty over some of the readings is mentioned in the notes below.

Bibliography

R. G. Ussher (ed.), *The Characters of Theophrastus* (London 1960) 135–157.

P. Steinmetz (ed.), *Theophrast, Charaktere*, II Kommentar und Übersetzung, (München 1962).

R. Parker, *Miasma* (Oxford 1983) 307.

J. Rusten (ed.), Theophrastus *Characters*, Loeb edition (Cambridge Mass. and London 2002).

Superstition would doubtless seem to be cowardice regarding the divine, and the superstitious man is the sort of person who, having washed his hands at a spring and sprinkled himself with water from a shrine, takes bay and puts it into his mouth and walks round the whole day
5   like that (5). And if a weasel runs across his path, he doesn't go on until someone crosses it or throws three stones over the path. And if he sees a snake in his house, if it's a reddish-brown one he calls on Sabazius, but if it's a sacred one he immediately builds a hero-shrine there. And on passing by some of the smooth stones at the crossroads
10   sacred to Hecate (10) he pours oil from his oil-flask onto them, and only goes away when he has fallen on his knees and kissed them. And if a mouse eats through his sack of barley-groats, he goes to the interpreter asking what he ought to do, and if he replies to him that he should hand it over to the cobbler to stitch up, he doesn't pay attention
15   to this advice but turns away and sacrifices. And he's even (15) prone to purifying his home frequently, saying a spell of Hecate has occurred. And if owls hoot when he's walking, he's terrified and only carries on having said 'Athene is stronger'. And he refuses either to approach a tomb or to go up to a corpse or a woman in childbirth, but asserts that
20   it's better for him not to be polluted (20). And on the fourth and seventh of the month, having instructed those inside to boil wine he goes out and buys myrtle-branches, frankincense and cakes, and coming inside again spends all day garlanding his statues of Hermaphroditus. And whenever he has a dream, he goes to the dream-interpreters, to the seers (25),
25   and to the bird-diviners in order to ask to which of the gods or to which goddess he should pray. And when he's about to be initiated into the mysteries he goes each month to the Orphic priests with his wife (and if his wife hasn't the time, with his nurse) and his children. And he would seem to be one of those who carefully purify themselves with water by
30   the sea (30). And if he ever sees one of the people at the crossroads garlanded with garlic, he goes away and washes his head and calls upon priestesses and tells them to purify him with squill or a puppy. And on seeing a madman or an epileptic he shudders and spits into his breast.

1 *Superstition ... divine*: the definition here, as elsewhere in the *Characters* may be an interpolation. Cowardice is not specifically mentioned in what follows.
doubtless: a favourite word of Theophrastus at the start of a character-sketch. First word in *Ch.* 13, 16, 23, 25; in the first sentence in 5, 18; at the start of a section at 2.9, 6.3, 19.3, 21.11, 24.12, 26.3, 27.5, 28.4, 30.18.

The fact that he does not confine its use to the start of a sketch tells against the idea that Theophrastus uses it (as Plato and Aristophanes do) to introduce his sketch as a reply to a previous question challenging him to define a particular character-type (so Ussher on 13.2 following Edmonds) and suggests it is more of a mannerism, idiosyncratic and colloquial and designed to reassure the reader, as some people today insist on beginning what they have to say with 'you know'.

Superstition: in Greek *deisidaimonia*, 'fear of the divine'. In Hesiod there was no suggestion that fearing the gods even over little things was bad, but by Theophrastus' time attitudes have changed and the attitude has pejorative connotations. This is the first extant use of the word *deisidaimonia*, and Theophrastus is also the first to use the adjective derived from it, *deisidaimon*, in a bad sense. Theophrastus' linguistic usage reflects change in religious attitudes. There is a rather different definition at the beginning of Plutarch's essay 'On Superstition' (*Moralia* 164e–171f), 'Naivety and ignorance concerning the gods' leading to the false belief that the gods cause one harm, though even Plutarch finds the actions of the superstitious man ridiculous (171e).

3 *spring*: a conjecture for the meaningless letters of the manuscripts; it seems suitably general for this opening example of superstition, and balances 'from a shrine' in the next clause, but the correct reading is quite uncertain.

4 *takes bay and puts it into his mouth*: bay was sacred to Apollo and used as an apotropaic. The superstitious man chews it so that Apollo will ward off evil spirits, perhaps through the effect on others of the smell of the chewed bay (cf. Parker, *Miasma* 228).

5 *a weasel*: a weasel crossing in front of one was a bad omen – cf. Ar. *Eccles.*792 where it is lumped together with earthquake and fire – as a black cat is sometimes nowadays.

6 *someone*: the idea is that if someone else comes along, they will take on the bad omen; if they do not come, stones will carry it away.

7 *reddish-brown one*: 'The pareas, or parouas, [snake] is red in colour, has sharp eyes and a wide mouth. Its bite is not harmful but gentle. Hence those who first discovered that it had these features consecrated it to the god who is kindliest to man and called it 'servant to Asclepius' (Aelian *NH* 8.12). Demosthenes (18.260) tells us that Aeschines brandished such snakes when celebrating what were probably the rites of Sabazius.

8 *Sabazius*: a Thraco-Phrygian god, assimilated to Dionysus and associated with snakes and informal rites; see R.Parker in *OCD*[3] s.v. Sabazius. The superstitious man over-reacts on seeing snakes: on seeing the harmless variety, he calls on a god; on seeing the venomous sort, he goes a step further and actually builds a shrine.

8 *a sacred one*: 'There is a certain very small snake, which some call sacred, which the really big snakes avoid. It grows to a cubit [= *c.* a foot] at most, and is hairy in appearance; whatever it bites is at once affected all over', Aristot. *HA* 607a).

9 *some of the smooth stones*: sc. sacred to Hecate, goddess of the crossroads. They are 'smooth' because regularly anointed, cf. Paus. 10.24.5: over a stone near the grave of Neoptolemus, the Delphians every day pour olive-oil and at each feast place on it unworked wool. See Burkert, *Greek Religion* 72: the oil makes the stones glisten.

11 *when he has fallen onto his knees and kissed them*: a very emotional reaction. The practice described is unusual for a Greek and generally foreign (A. *Pers*. 499 Persians, Hdt. 2.121 Egyptians). Greeks did not normally kneel down in worship, but stood with outstretched arms (Burkert, *Greek Religion* 75). See further, S. Pulleyn, *Prayer in Greek Religion* (Oxford 1997) 188–95.

12 *mouse*: the Greek word could also mean 'rat'.

13 *interpreter*: unofficial religious person; cf. 25–6 below: the superstitious man seeks advice from a variety of interpreters. His milieu is the world of local, popular, unofficial religion, so it is unlikely that by 'interpreter' Theophrastus means a state official, such as one of the Eumolpidae (so Steinmetz, 192), nor does the reply of the interpreter support such an interpretation.

15 *sacrifices*: a conjecture. He averts the omen by sacrificing. He is so superstitious that he does not accept the interpreter's practical advice, but insists on doing something that will lessen his irrational fear of being harmed by the gods.

16 *to purifying*: he seems to believe a sorcerer has conjured the goddess into his house, and that she must be exorcised – a drastic reaction (Parker, *Miasma* 222–3). Purification, often by water or fire, was the standard way to deal with pollution from disease or bewitchment.

Hecate: goddess of magic. There is a very thorough article on her by Henrichs in *OCD*[3].

17–18 *And if owls hoot ... 'Athene is stronger'*: the underlying idea seems to be that when out on a journey the superstitious man hears owls hoot; in his state of fear he takes the noise as a bad omen (cf. Hes. *Op*. 747: a crow cawing on your roof is a bad omen), but is able to continue, comforting himself with the thought that Athene is stronger than they are and will protect him. But both text and interpretation are uncertain.

18–21 It is possible that Theophrastus has Hesiod in mind here: bird noise as omen, pollution from tombs, the 4th and 7th of the month, are all paralleled in *Op*.

18–20 *And he refuses ... polluted*: he is racked by fear of pollution, so avoids contact with birth, death and tombs, three standard sources of impurity and pollution (Parker, *Miasma* ch.2) and hence of divine wrath if contact with them is made. For tombs, cf. Hes. *Op*. 735, 750.

20–3 *And on the fourth and seventh ... Hermaphroditus*: a difficult passage. Taboos concerning days were widespread in the ancient world (see West *Op*. pp. 348–9). The fourth of the month was the birthday of Hermes and Aphrodite, the seventh Apollo's birthday (West on *Op*. 770). The idea seems to be that the superstitious man goes so far as to take a holiday on these holy days, perform a sacrifice, and garland his Hermaphrodites, giving days of minor religious significance the accord of a major festival.

21 *to boil wine*: a strange instruction, but perhaps either to make it stronger for a festival by boiling off the water with which it was mixed, or to create a smell as part of a fumigation/purification process (cf. below on **22**).

22 *frankincense and cakes*: an emendation for the manuscripts' 'plate of a number of pieces of frankincense', where the plural 'number of pieces of frankincense' is odd, though, if the superstitious man is fumigating, a plate of lots of frankincense might be useful.

23 *Hermaphroditus*: a half-male, half-female deity whose cult at Athens is first attested in the fourth century. Why should the superstitious man worship him/her on the fourth and seventh days of the month in particular? We should not seek too rational an explanation (after all, by definition most of his superstitious reactions are irrational): it is enough for him that Hermes and Aphrodite have special connections with the fourth (see on **20–3**), and that the fourth and seventh go together in Hesiod's *Op.* to which Theophrastus probably alludes in this character sketch (see on **18–21**).

We know too little about the cult of Hermaphroditus to justify emending away the reference to Hermaphroditus here ('statues of Hermes', Steinmetz). The superstitious man is clearly in a jumpy mood, going from inside the house to outside, then inside again – from the women's domain to the men's – and his choice of Hermaphroditus may be influenced by this.

23–6 He takes any dream as a bad omen, and has to have it interpreted so as to know to which god or goddess he should pray in order to avert the impending evil. And he goes to three classes of diviners, just as (if the emendation above, **22**, is accepted) he purchased three sacrificial items and avoided pollution from three sources (**18–20**). Literary style more than anything else lies behind this, especially as in practice a seer might also be a bird-diviner (cf. Teiresias, S. *OT.* 999). His visits to these various experts show that there was a substantial industry in interpreting omens in Hellenistic times.

26–8 *And when ... his children*: anxious that nothing should go wrong at any initiation ceremony, he takes the precaution of visiting experts in Orphic rites who would readily (for a fee) claim to be able to counsel him about initiation ceremonies. On monthly instruction for initiation candidates, see J. Morrison *CR* 15 (1965) 289.

27 *Orphic priests*: itinerant experts in mystery religion (cf. Plato *Rep.* 346b–d). The superstitious man, facing imminent initiation into a mystery cult, is worried (as usual) in case there might be a reason why his initiation might offend the god of the cult, so he goes to the Orphic experts who claimed to be able by various dubious means to avert divine anger. Orphic priests would have been particularly useful for him as, contrary to more bona fide mystery cults, they published their advice in book form (cf. Burkert, *Greek Religion* 297).

29 *one of those who purify themselves with water*: cf. **2–5**, **16** above for his over-concern with purification. He does not merely purify himself with a sprinkling of water, but apparently in his desperate anxiety 'repeatedly undergoes ablution in the sea' (Parker, *Miasma* 307, though the Greek contains no word for 'repeatedly'). Sea-water was particularly valued for its purificatory effects (*Miasma* 226–7).

31 *garlanded*: a conjecture; garlic was an apotropaic, used to ward off the evil eye, so the idea would seem to be that the superstitious man infers from what he sees that an evil spirit is present. But why 'garlanded'? Hence Jebb's suggestion, 'feasting on garlic', *i.e.* he sees someone eating offerings of garlic meant for Hecate: 'The superstitious man holds that he has been defiled by the mere sight of such wickedness' (Jebb ad loc.). A variety of food offerings were left for Hecate, but garlic is not mentioned elsewhere. However, the general point is clear: he overreacts, and regards a comic, pitiful scene as a bad omen and seeks to avert the evil.

32 *to purify him with squill or a puppy*: the puppy is whipped and sacrificed, and the superstitious man purified with its blood: in his desperate attempt to avert divine ill-will, he resorts to a major blood-sacrifice by a priestess (see *Miasma* ch.7, esp. p.230: 'the most despised of animals was used to receive the candidate's impurity'). The idea was that the impure person comes into contact with the animal's blood, which is then washed away, thus ridding him of any source of guilt (*Miasma* 373). The squill (a plant) may have been used in a similar way, the person whipped with it until he bled and the blood then washed away (*Miasma* 231–2).

33 Both the madman and the epileptic are regarded by the superstitious man, as by most Greeks, as afflicted by a god; the sight of them, therefore, is interpreted by him as a bad omen from a god, to be averted by spitting, an apotropaic practice (cf. on **4** above).

4. Herodotus 6. 105–106: A Divine Epiphany (Pheidippides and Pan)

This divine epiphany (n.b. 106.**2** 'when he said Pan *appeared* to him') occurred during the Persian Wars in 490 BC. The Athenians sent Pheidippides, a specialist ultra-distance runner who could run all day, to Sparta (246 kilometers, *c.* 154 miles) to obtain Spartan help for warding off the Persians who had reached Marathon. On the way, in the Arcadian countryside, Pan appeared to him and asked why he (Pan) was not worshipped at Athens despite his friendliness towards the Athenians. Subsequently, Herodotus says, the Athenians did worship Pan, with annual sacrifices and a torch-race. After setting out from Athens Pheidippides arrived in Sparta the very next day. Having listened to Pheidippides' request, the Spartans procrastinated for religious reasons, eventually ariving at Marathon after the battle was over (Hdt. 6.120). What happened to Pheidippides we are not told by Herodotus. The story which has given rise to the modern marathon, that he ran from Marathon to Athens to announce the Greek victory over the Persians and promptly expired, is told by Lucian (63.4) more than 600 years after the event. A modern race is run over the distance, the Spartathlon. The record for the event is 20 hours 25 minutes set in 1984 by Jannis Kouros a Greek, so it is not impossible that Pheidippides did indeed arrive in Sparta the day after setting out from Athens.

Herodotus' account is succinct and matter-of-fact. It conceals a number of different elements:

1 It is an aetiological story, providing an explanation for why the cult of Pan at Athens started only after the time of the Battle of Marathon. Archaeological evidence supports this chronology, with many caves dedicated to Pan and nymphs coming into existence in Attica in the early fifth century (see R. Parker, *Athenian Religion: A History* (Oxford, 1996), 163–8 esp. 164–5).

2 The story provides Herodotus with the opportunity to provide an explanation, not uncomplimentary to the Spartans, for why they did not help the Athenians at Marathon.

3 The epiphany occurred during a time of war; hence it can be classified as a 'military epiphany', a type well documented and much discussed. In Herodotus miraculous apparitions of gods, heroes or humans are particularly common during, or prior to, battles, because then especially unexpected turns of events may happen which the intense excitement of warfare makes especially susceptible to explanation in terms of supernatural intervention. The Persian Wars is a period when epiphanies were numerous, just because defeat of the Persians against the odds was explicable only on the assumption of divine help. Pheidippides' encounter with Pan, a divinity favourable to the Athenians, is a precursor to unexpected disaster for the Persians. Something comparable may underlie Thucydides 4.116 where Brasidas, after unexpectedly capturing a fort at Lecythus, gave 30 minae to Athene, who had a temple nearby, and turned the place into a sacred precinct, 'having reckoned that the capture had occurred by some more than human power'; the implication is that Brasidas believed that Athene had intervened in the siege (see Hornblower's commentary ad loc.), though unlike the Pheidippides episode and in keeping with Thucydides' generally not resorting to the gods as explanations, there is no specific mention of an epiphany.

4 The episode explains how Pheidippides managed to accomplish his journey so quickly (106.**2–3** he 'was in Sparta the day after he left the city of Athens'): he was an Athenian and, as such, favoured by Pan's general goodwill towards the Athenians. Pheidippides is tantamount to a successful athlete, so it is natural for him to be credited with having received divine help. Since his journey from Athens to Sparta went

through Arcadia where Pan was particularly worshipped, and since Herodotus wants to slip in 1. above (the aetiology of Pan's post-Marathon cult in Athens), Pan is the obvious choice of deity.

Speculation about psychological explanations for Pheidippides' vision abound. Garland (50) suggests that Pheidippides may have been hallucinating from exhaustion *etc.*, Parker (167) that 'he felt himself far and frighteningly removed from his own familiar home' and was thus appropriately confronted by Pan the god of the countryside and of panic. But there is none of this in Herodotus. What Herodotus does mention is that Pheidippides was a trained professional, thus fit for the job.

Bibliography

W. K. Pritchett, *The Greek States at War* lll (California 1979) 1–46 esp. 23–4.

R. Garland, *Introducing New Gods* (London 1992) 47–63.

J. Gould, 'Herodotus and Religion' in *Greek Historiography* ed. S. Hornblower (Oxford 1994) 91–106.

T. Harrison, *Divinity and History: The Religion of Herodotus* (Oxford 2000) ch. 3, 64–101, 'Miracles and the Miraculous'.

105

And first, while they were still in the city, the generals dispatched to Sparta a messenger called Pheidippides, an Athenian who specialised in running all day and trained for this. As Pheidippides himself said when he reported back to the Athenians, when he was around Mt. Parthenium

5   above Tegea the god Pan suddenly appeared to him. (2) Shouting out his name 'Pheidippides' Pan told him to report back to the Athenians and ask them why they paid him no attention when he was friendly to the Athenians and had often in the past been of service to them and moreover would be in the future. (3) The Athenians, since their affairs

10   were by now in good order, believed what he said to be true and built a shrine to Pan beneath the Acropolis and from the time of Pheidippides' account worshipped Pan with annual sacrifices and a torch-race.

106

This man Pheidippides, when he had been sent by the generals on the occasion when he said Pan appeared to him, was in Sparta the day after he left the city of Athens, and having arrived in the presence of the authorities he said: (2) 'Spartans, the Athenians need you to help

5   them and not to look on while their city, the oldest in Greece, falls into slavery at the hands of barbarians. For even now Eretria has been enslaved and Greece has become weaker by one famous city.' (2) So he announced to them as he had been instructed, and they were happy to help the Athenians but it was impossible for them to do so straightaway

10   as they did not wish to break their law; for it was the ninth day of the month and they said they could not march out since it was not a full moon.

105

1 *in the city*: Athens, before setting out for Marathon to confront the Persians.

2 *Pheidippides*: his name may have been Philippides. Pheidippides has the support of the better family of manuscripts, the latter of most later authors recalling the runner – but, perhaps crucially, not Nepos, the Roman historian of the 1st century BC (*Vit. Milt.* 4.3), the next author after Herodotus to mention the runner. Philippides is the commoner name.

2–3 *who specialised in running all day*: sc. during daylight hours, *c.* 13, as the Battle of Marathon took place in September – v. N. G. L. Hammond, *JHS* 88 (1968), 37–40. If he set out at dawn on day 1, and arrived in Sparta at dusk the following day (see 106.2), he would have had about 26 hours of daylight running. The modern record for the distance is 20 hours 25 minutes (see Introduction above).

    Each Greek city seems to have had its own corps of ultra-distance day-runners (*hemerodromoi*); cf. Herodotus 9.12 and V. J. Matthews, *CW* 68 (1974), 161–9.

3 *As Pheidippides himself said ...*: Pheidippides' account is Herodotus' source for the story.

4–5 *around Mt. Parthenium above Tegea*: Greek mountains were notoriously numinous, and provided the homes and haunts of gods and goddesses. Pausanias (8.54.6) thought he could identify the sanctuary to Pan on Mt. Parthenium where the encounter took place. Pan was a god of the countryside and especially worshipped in Arcadia.

7–9 *when he was friendly to the Athenians ... and would be in the future*: this benevolence is not recorded elsewhere.

12 *torch-race*: either a straight running race holding a torch, or relay race with the torch as a baton (see How and Wells on Herodotus 8.98.2).

106

6 *Eretria*: in Euboea.

9–10 *it was impossible for them to do so ... break their law*: a cryptic reference to the Carnea festival, held 7th–15th (*i.e.* up until the full-moon) of the month Metageitnion (August/September), during which time all Dorians abstained from warfare.

5. Aeschylus *Agamemnon* 160–183: Hymn to Zeus

This hymn to Zeus comes in the first choral song of Aeschylus' *Agamemnon*, the first play of his Oresteia trilogy. It recalls hymns used in actual worship, in its emphasis on the importance of calling the god by his right name, and in its detailing of the god's rise to power and nature of his powers (v. Lloyd-Jones on 160). Gods were regularly invoked in times of stress and anxiety, so it is appropriate that Zeus is invoked at some length here in the play as we await Agamemnon's return to Clytemestra: the invocation builds up tension early in the play and thereby creates issues which the rest of the trilogy will unfold. The old men who form the chorus here are, because of their physical powerlessness, anxious: they know of the background to the expedition against Troy, and now after ten years they are roused by Clytemestra's appearance (82) and the blazing altars she has kindled (86–91) to recollect immediately following this hymn the disturbing events that took place at Aulis, especially Agamemnon's sacrifice of his daughter Iphigeneia (184–257). Zeus in particular is invoked because it was he who sent the Greeks against the Trojans following Paris' transgression in abducting Helen (60ff., 118ff.) and he who thereby roused the anger of the pro-Trojan goddess Artemis. So Agamemnon in bringing about justice commits injustice (as Orestes does later, in the second play of the trilogy the *Libation Bearers*). It is the consequences of his injustice that the chorus are worried about and lead them now to call on Zeus (see Denniston and Page, xxiii–xxix).

Bibliography

J. D. Denniston and D. L. Page (eds), *Aeschylus: Agamemnon* (Oxford 1957).
P. H. Lloyd-Jones, *Agamemnon by Aeschylus* (New Jersey 1970).
P. M. Smith, *On the Hymn to Zeus in Aeschylus' Agamemnon* (Chicago 1980).
R. C. T. Parker, 'hymns (Greek)' in *Oxford Classical Dictionary*[3] (Oxford 1996).

Zeus, whoever he is, if he likes being called by this name, I call him this. Weighing everything up, I cannot liken him to anything except Zeus, if I must really cast the idle burden from my mind. (165).

5   Nor the one who before was great, brimming with almighty boldness, not even he will be spoken of since he lived before (170). And he who was next born has gone, having met with a victorious opponent. Someone enthusiastically shouting a victory song to Zeus will completely hit the mark of sense (175),

Zeus who put mortals on the way to understanding, who validated
10 'learning through suffering'. Instead of sleep there drips before the
heart toil mindful of pain (180): sense comes even to those who do not
want it. The favour of the gods, sitting on their holy seats, is, I suppose,
one that comes by force.

1–2 *Zeus ... I call him this*: 'Whoever Zeus is, if he likes to be called this (sc. 'Zeus'),
I call him this ('Zeus'). The opening is characteristically hymnic: cf. Sappho 1.1–7,
'Aphrodite ... I beg you ... come here, if ever before you heard my prayers'.
2–3 *Weighing everything up ... from my mind*: the precise interpretation is uncertain,
but the general sense is, 'I cannot liken Zeus to anything except Zeus, *i.e.* Zeus is
incomparable (as a source of relief), and that I must accept, if I am to rid myself of
this idle burden of anxiety.'
4–8 *Nor the one who before was great ... hit the mark of sense*: Zeus' predecessors,
Uranus and Cronus, have gone; Zeus is now in power; so I must turn to Zeus.
An account of the deity's rise to power is another standard hymnic feature. The
succession myth (best known from Hesiod's *Theogony* in which Cronus castrated
Uranus, and Zeus in turn overthrew Cronus) is particularly relevant to the House of
Atreus with its succession of rulers and struggles for power.
6 *victorious opponent*: Zeus. The Greek literally means one who wins in a wrestling
competition by throwing his opponent three times. In this passage Aeschylus is
depicting the succession myth in terms of athletics victories.
9–13 Zeus takes one along the road to understanding; the road to understanding is
arrived at by learning through bitter experience; the learning process is painful and
unrelaxing; it comes forcibly even to those who don't want it.
10 *'learning through suffering'*: a proverbial expression, cf. Herodotus 1.207. The
proverb applies loosely to the *Oresteia* in general: a harsh lesson is dealt to the
Trojans, Paris, Agamemnon and Clytemnestra; they learn that Zeus punishes the
unjust, and others can learn from their example. Cf. also 250, 'Justice comes down
on people so that they learn through suffering'.

6. Pindar *Pythian* Ten: The Victorious Athlete and the Divine

Pythian 10 is Pindar's earliest surviving victory-ode. It was composed for
Hippocleas from Thessaly who had won the boys' diaulos running race (see
on **9**) at the Pythian Games in 498 B.C. Although the precise meaning of
some of the Greek is uncertain, as is the case with all the odes of Pindar
because of his allusive and contrived style, the ode contains in clear form a
number of his central tenets regarding man's relationship to the gods.
The first is that success in athletics requires both inherited natural ability

and help from the gods (**10–12**). Pindar's ideology recognises that to be successful at the highest level an athlete, even a naturally talented athlete, needs factors outside his control to be favourable.

Secondly, a successful athlete because of his elevated status is *ipso facto* all the more prone to a reversal of fortune, if he should overstep the mark and the gods should come to resent his good fortune. Pindar regularly refers to the precarious position of a victorious athlete, someone who is in closer contact with the gods than ordinary mortals because of his display of superhuman prowess but thereby all the more prone to downfall (**19–22**).

Thirdly, just as Pindar, an inspired poet, gets his inspiration from the divine Muses (**65**), so too through his divinely inspired praise of the victor he can bestow a type of non-controversial immortality on him through the immortality of song. He alludes to these relationships in the myth. The blessed and unageing Hyperboreans have the music and dances of the Muses among them; by implication, the victor too who is celebrated amid the poetry of the Muses is blessed and has a kind of immortality.

Lastly, although the victor has affinities with the divine, he must always realise his limitations as a mortal (see on **29–54**).

The poem, then, illustrates how through superhuman athletic success one can temporarily approach the divine. Victorious athletes, especially those victorious in the boxing, wrestling or pancration at the Olympics, were regarded as having performed superhuman deeds. Generally, their rewards were limited to money and privileges from their home city, but an occasional few were actually worshipped as heroes (so Cleomedes, Paus. 6.9.8) or even gods (Theagenes, Paus. 6.11.8).

Bibliography

R. W. B. Burton, *Pindar's Pythian Odes* (Oxford 1962) 1–14.

A. Köhnken, *Die Funktion des Mythos bei Pindar* (Berlin/New York 1971) 154–187.

S. Instone, *Pindar: Selected Odes* (Warminster 1996) 1–30.

Sparta is prosperous, Thessaly blessed. The family of Heracles peerless in battle, descended from a single father, rules over both. Why do I boast inappropriately? But Pytho and Pelinnaion and the sons of Aleuas call me, wanting me to bring to Hippocleas (5) the resounding encomiastic

5   voice of men. For he tastes the delight of the victory-prize and the nook of Parnassus proclaimed him to the crowd of those dwelling nearby as

supreme among the boy diaulos-runners. Apollo, when a god is helping, sweet grows men's beginning and their goal (10). He has achieved this thanks in some degree to your efforts, but his inherited ability has trod in

10 the footsteps of his father, twice an Olympic victor in the war-sustaining weapons of Ares; for the deep-meadowed contest beneath the rocks of Cirrha (15) made Phricias too victorious in the footrace. May fate follow so that in later days too proud wealth flourishes for them.

Having received as their share no small gift of the sweet things in
15 Greece, may they not meet with jealous reversals from the gods (20). May god be unpained at heart, but for poets this man becomes blessed and worthy of song, whoever having been victorious with his hands or excellence of foot takes the greatest of prizes with daring and strength, and still lives (25) to see his young son rightfully getting Pythian crowns. But
20 the bronze heaven is never able to be climbed by him. Yet, as to what glories we mortal people do attain, he goes on the furthest sailing. But neither by ship nor on foot travelling would you find the wondrous way to the throng of the Hyperboreans (30), with whom the leader Perseus once feasted on going to their homes, encountering them sacrificing
25 glorious hecatombs of asses to the god. In their continuous festivities and worship Apollo especially rejoices (35), and he laughs on seeing the upright arrogance of the monsters.

And the Muse is not absent from their ways, but everywhere choruses of girls and the noises of lyres and the sharp sounds of pipes ring out; and
30 having bound their hair with golden laurel (40) they feast cheerfully. Neither illnesses nor destructive old-age mixes with this sacred race, but they live without toils and battles escaping punishment for injustice. Breathing with a bold heart, the son of Danaë once came to this crowd of blessed men, and Athene guided him (45). And he killed the Gorgon,
35 and with her head woven with the locks of snakes he came bearing a stony death to islanders. When the gods accomplish it, nothing ever seems too incredible for me to wonder (50). Loosen your grip on the oar, quickly thrust the anchor from the prow onto land, a defence against a rocky reef. For the pick of encomiastic songs darts from one theme to
40 another.

I hope (55), with the Ephyraeans pouring out my sweet voice around Peneion, to make with my songs Hippocleas, thanks to his victory-crowns, even more beautiful among those of his own age and among his elders too, and a darling for young girls. For loves for different things

45   chafe the mind of different people (60); what things each person yearns
for, he will get, and hold onto as a graspable object of his desire, the one
close at hand. But what lies a year ahead is baffling to foresee. I trust the
kind hospitality of Thorax who, conducting pleasurable business for me,
yoked this four-horse chariot of the Muses (65), a friend for a friend,
50   kindly guiding me as I guide it. For one experiencing it, both gold when
put to the test and an upright mind shine out. And we shall praise noble
brothers, because they bear high and exalt the law of the Thessalians
(70). The careful government of a country's cities depends on noble
men.

1 *Sparta is prosperous, Thessaly blessed*: the loftier of the two epithets, 'blessed',
with connotations of divinity, is naturally applied to Thessaly where the quasi-
divine victor lives. Pindar likes these striking, elliptical beginnings to odes, cf.
O. 1.1 'Water is best'. The mention of Sparta here is probably an allusion to the
political situation shortly before the composition of *P.* 10 when Thessaly allied
herself with Sparta against Athens.

1–2 The descendants of Heracles, who are descended from a single ancestor
(Heracles), rule over both Sparta and Thessaly. Heracles' descendants spread
themselves all over Greece; Pindar singles out their branches at Sparta and Thessaly
because of the context of this particular ode.

2–3 *Why do I boast inappropriately?*: Pindar pretends that he has said something
inappropriate, but he is speaking tongue-in-cheek because, as the next lines show,
his mention of Heracles was really wholly appropriate because it links the victor
with Heracles, implying that the victor has inherited Heracles' athletic prowess and
thereby adding to the victor's glory.

3 *Pytho*: *i.e.* Delphi, where the Pythian Games were held.

Pellinnaion: the name of the victor's hometown.

sons of Aleuas: the Aleuadae, a powerful, aristocratic family of Thessaly who had
commissioned the ode for Hippocleas.

4–5 *encomiastic voice of men*: the 'men' are the chorus who sung *P.* 10.

6 *Parnassus*: mountain overlooking Delphi. A herald would have announced Hippocleas
as victor.

7 *diaulos-runners*: the diaulos was a running race two lengths of the stadium, there
and back, a little less than 400m.

7–8 *Apollo ... goal*: you need the help of the gods for success. Apollo, who presided
over the Pythian Games, has helped Hippocleas to be successful.

beginning and ... goal: a 'polar' expression, giving the two poles (or extremes) of
a continuum. So here 'men's end and beginning' means the whole range of activity
undertaken by men, *i.e.* (in this context) Hippocleas' participation in the games and
victory.

9–10 Where appropriate Pindar regularly stresses how victors follow their forebears' footsteps: he thought inherited natural ability as important for success as divine favour.

10–11 *his father ...Ares*: the father was twice a victor at Olympia in the race in armour, a length of the stadium and back with helmet, shield and perhaps greaves. The son won in the there-and-back race without armour, showing he had inherited his father's ability at that distance.

11–12 *and the deep-meadowed ... footrace*: Hippocleas' father, Phricias, had won a running event at the Pythian Games too.

12 *Cirrha*: port near where the Pythian Games were held.

12–13 *May fate ... for them*: 'may they be successful in the future and not meet with reversals of fortune'. Pindar rightly reckons that the family, because of its success so far, is especially prone to a future reversal.

13 *wealth*: 'wealth' here means success and the wealth which success brings. Winners at the major Games could end up receiving substantial rewards.

14–15 *Having received ... gods*: the gods are jealous of success. The athlete was in a dilemma: to be successful, he needed the help of the gods; but that very success could rouse the jealousy of the gods (who did not like to see mortals overstepping their mortal limits) and hence cause the gods to begrudge further success.

15–17 *May god ... song*: interpretation of the Greek, and the connection of thought between the two clauses is disputed. The most plausible interpretation is, 'May god be unpained at heart [and not harbour, because of the family's success, the ill-feeling mentioned in **15**,'jealous reversals from the gods']: in the eyes of poets a man who has won in the games becomes blessed and worthy of song [and not deserving of divine ill-feeling].' Thus the central thought is that although the gods may possibly be anxious about the consequences of the victor's success, for the poet there is no question about his deserts.

16–19 *this man ... whoever ... Pythian crowns*: the sentence begins by seeming to have a general reference to any victorious athlete, but as it progresses it comes to refer to the father and son victors for whom the present ode was composed.

20–1 *Yet, as to what ... furthest sailing*: the victor obtains the highest of those glories we do obtain.

23–36 The Myth of Perseus among the Hyperboreans.

The Hyperboreans, a fantastic people of the far north, live in a blessed condition, analogous to that of the victor, but they can never really be reached by human beings. So they serve to underline both the special status of the victor and also his limitations. The fact that Perseus, with divine help, once went to them and then returned, highlights another aspect of the victor: his bliss is ephemeral (because for all his success the future is uncertain). Pindar describes the Hyperboreans subtly, both to allude to the victor and to contrast with him: they have music and garlands and feasting (as the celebrating victor does), but they lack disease, old-age and hardship (not true of the victor).

23 *throng*: in Greek the word can also mean 'contest', as in **11** above; Pindar thereby introduces the Hyperboreans with a word designed to encourage one to see in them allusions to the victor.

23 *the leader Perseus*: Perseus is a leader of people, as are the Aleuadae.

once: no one in Pindar's day could do what Perseus did.

25–30 The Hyperboreans' festivities match those of the victor, and their connections with Apollo are relevant to the fact that this ode is for a victory in the Pythian Games held in Apollo's honour.

26–7 *and he laughs on seeing the upright arrogance of the monsters*: interpretation is disputed, but most see in 'upright arrogance' an allusion to the asses having erections. But the point of such an allusion, apart from it adding to the joviality of the occasion, is unclear.

28–30 Dancing and music, and a feast, would be part of the victor's celebrations too.

30 *golden laurel*: victors in the Pythian Games received a laurel wreath, but the Hyperboreans' laurel wreaths are gold because divine and everlasting.

31–2 The Hyperboreans live without the ills that commonly beset men.

32 *but they live ... injustice*: the idea seems to be that since struggle and war play no part in their lives, they can live peaceably, having put away the need for the sort of excessive revenge that is often found among humans in times of strife.

33 *son of Danaë*: Perseus.

34–6 *And he killed the gorgon ... death to islanders*: Pindar briefly touches on the most amazing of all Perseus' achievements, his killing of the Gorgon Medusa and bringing back of her snakey head to the island of Seriphos where his mother was enslaved; when he showed the head to the islanders and their king Polydectes, they were turned to stone and his mother freed (the story is told more fully at *P.* 12.11–17). Pindar dwells in this ode on Perseus among the Hyperboreans, because that episode provides most allusions to the victor's felicity, but he touches on the famous Medusa myth, because that leads up to the gnomic statement of lines **36–7** on the power of the gods to help one to amazing success, which in turn reminds us of line **7** above where Pindar highlighted how the victor's success was due to divine assistance.

37–9 Pindar often uses vivid metaphors of this sort as a means of moving on from one topic to another, cf. *P.* 11.38–40 'Earlier on I was going the right way, when I got thrown into confusion at the crossroads. Or did some wind throw me off-course as if I were a little boat at sea?'

38–9 *a defence against a rocky reef*: secure anchorage prevents shipwreck. Likewise Pindar, if he returns to familiar themes, will not get carried away into irrelevance.

39–40 *For the pick ... another*: Pindar means that his odes contain a variety of themes and he must not dwell too long on any single one of them. The bee image is particularly appropriate, as Pindar's poetry is honey-sweet for the victor.

41–2 *I hope ... Peneion*: The Thessalians who inhabited the victor's city of Pelinnaion

(3), near Mt. Peneion, were men of Ephyra, probably an old name for the Thessalian city of Kranon, and they supplied the chorus that performed *P*. 10.

44 *a darling for young girls*: Pindar quite often in odes for young victors stresses that they will be admired by the girls: a young, victorious male would make an attractive future husband.

44–7 *For loves ... close at hand*: different people yearn for different things. To succeed in getting what one wants, one should focus on what is readily available. This is a common piece of Pindaric advice, and in the context of this poem as a whole suggests that the victorious athlete should not aspire to the impossible.

48 Thorax was head of the Aleuadae family and had commissioned the ode.

47–50 *I trust ... as I guide it*: Thorax is friendly towards Pindar, Pindar friendly towards Thorax; Thorax guides (*i.e.* encourages) Pindar, Pindar, inspired by the Muses, guides the Muses' chariot (*i.e.* composes the ode). The strained language alludes to the fact that Pindar's ode was produced in return for money.

50–1 *For one experiencing it ... shine out*: 'An upright mind shines out for one who is experiencing it, just as true gold when put to the test shines true for an expert'. The first part of the sentence alludes to Pindar's experience of Thorax's fairness and hospitality.

51–2 *noble brothers*: Thorax, Euryphilus and Thrasydaeus, who uphold law among the Thessalians.

53 *noble men*: *i.e.* the aforementioned brothers.

7. Empedocles, selected fragments: The Divine Forces of Love and Strife; Metempsychosis and the Divine

Empedocles is one of the most bizarre of the Presocratic philosophers. His philosophy, written as poetry, survives only in fragments and interpretation is often disputed, but the following account probably gives the gist of his thought. He believed that the universe was, and will be, dominated by two divine forces, Love and Strife, which wax and wane alternately. Under this everlasting cosmic cycle the divine elements (fire, water, earth, air) alternately come together (under the rule of Love) and fragment (under Strife), and objects in the world are formed and dissolve. Under maximum Love (and minimum Strife) they come together to such an extent that all that exists is a ball of divine Love.

There is also an ethical side to Empedocles' philosophy. Given that Love and Strife make everything in the world, they also make us human beings, and Empedocles seems to have explained this in conjunction with a belief in Pythagorean metempsychosis, which was particularly popular in southern Italy and Sicily (where he lived). According to this belief, people's souls are reincarnated in response to how they have lived their lives: into higher forms of life, ultimately becoming divine, following good behaviour, and into lower forms following a wicked life. As the force of Love is increasing to its maximum, so we mortals live more and more harmoniously and with increasing love, ultimately becoming part of the one divine sphere of Love. When the divine sphere breaks up through Strife, we lose our divine nature and embark on a fall. Empedocles thought that cosmic Strife manifests itself within human behaviour in sacrifice, especially animal sacrifice, believing like the followers of Pythagoras that all living beings are akin and (most radically) that ritual slaughter, which most Greeks accepted without demur, is immoral.

In addition, one's mind too is holy and divine. How this fits in with the physics and ethics mentioned above is unclear, but perhaps Empedocles believed that the fall in status of the soul was accompanied by, or analogous to, a downgrading of the use of mind, in particular that the strife involved in sacrifice, that causes man to quit the blessed realm of divine love, is based on a failure to see the truth, as would happen if pure mind is invaded by impure and erroneous beliefs. If this account is correct, then we see here a theory that equates maximal use of intelligence with maximal divinity and maximal happiness (cf. below, Aristotle on *theoria*).

Such, in outline, seems to be what he thought, but much is uncertain. It used to be thought that he wrote two separate poems, *Physics* and *Purifications*, but a recent papyrus discovery (see A. Martin and O. Primavesi (eds) in Bibliography below) suggests that there may only ever have been one poem and that the ethics (or some of it) prefaced the physics, the cycle of the soul's reincarnations being in the physics put into its larger, cosmic context.

What Empedocles seems to have thought is that, given we are made of divine elements, we at all times have a divine nature, but that only when the elements totally combine under maximal Love do we share in godliness. The idea that divinity is in the very fabric of the world is not new: the Homeric gods pervade the world as powerful forces, and Thales famously said 'The world is full of gods', adducing the uncanny power a magnet has to attract iron. What seems to have led Empedocles to put more emphasis on human divinity is his sympathy with Pythagoreanism and the belief that our mortal fabric is essentially the same as the divine fabric of the universe.

There are many problems of interpretation with all this. In what sense do we preserve any identity as we metamorphose from fragmented elements to part of the god-sphere of Love? Are we currently moving towards total Love and unity, or towards total Strife? And if Strife is a god, are we any less divine or godlike when total Strife reigns? In one fragment (112.4–5, quoted below) Empedocles claims he is an immortal, no longer a mortal. This status would seem to require that Love is reigning supreme. But how can that be the case in our, and Empedocles', messy and sinful world? And if it is the case, given that total Love is nothing but a homogenous sphere, how can Empedocles speak at all? Perhaps Empedocles claimed special status, but to what extent he addressed these questions is uncertain because of the fragmentary nature of the text.

Bibliography

A. Martin and O. Primavesi, *L'Empédocle de Strasbourg* (Berlin 1999), English summary 339–348.

C. Osborne, 'Rummaging in the Recycling Bins of Upper Egypt: A Discussion of A. Martin and O. Primavesi, *L'Empédocle de Strasbourg'*, *Oxford Studies in Classical Philosophy* 18 (2000) 329– 356.

M. R. Wright (ed.), *Empedocles: the Extant Fragments* (revised edition London 1995).

Fragments 115–137 below are ethical in content, fragments 6–31 + 134 physical.

Fr. 115

There is an oracle of Necessity, an ancient decree of the gods, eternal, sealed with broad oaths, that, whenever one pollutes his own limbs with the blood of slaughter, and whoever has committed a sin in strife and swears a false oath, one of the gods who have obtained a share of blessed
5 life (5), they have to wander away from the blessed ones for thrice ten thousand seasons, growing in time into all kinds of mortal forms that are changing their painful ways of life. For the strength of the air pursues him seawards, and the sea spits him out onto the surface of the earth, and the land into the rays (10) of the shining sun, and he into the eddies
10 of the sky. They receive him from each other, and all hate him. I too am now one of them, an exile from the gods and a wanderer, having put my trust in mad strife.

Fr. 117

For I have already in the past become a boy and a girl and a bush and a bird and a dumb fish from the sea.

Fr. 112

O friends who dwell on the acropolis in the great city that comes down from golden Acragas, carers of good deeds, respectful harbours for foreigners, with no experience in evil, rejoice, I walk honoured among you all as an immortal god, no longer a mortal, as I believe (5), garlanded
5   with ribbons and blooming crowns. Whenever I come to flourishing cities, I am honoured by men and women; they follow with me in countless numbers asking in what direction is the road to gain, some needing oracles and others (10) inquired to hear a healing utterance for all sorts of diseases being long pierced with grievous pains.

Fr. 127

Among wild beasts they become ground-sleeping mountain lions, and bays among beautiful-leafed trees.

Fr. 146

And finally they are seers and songsters and doctors and chiefs among men on earth, whence they grow up as gods supreme in honours.

Fr. 147

Sharing a hearth with the other immortals, being at the same table, with no part in the woes of men, indestructible.

Fr. 130

There were all tame things kind to mankind, wild beasts and birds, and friendliness shone forth.

Fr. 135

But the law for everything is drawn continuously through the wide-ruling sky and through the boundless light.

Fr. 139

Alas that a pitiless day did not destroy me before I devised with my claws wretched deeds for food.

Fr. 136

Will you not cease from ill-sounding slaughter? Do you not see that it is one another that you are devouring through your carelessness of mind?

Fr. 137

A father lifts up his dear son, who has changed shape, and praying kills him, great fool. And they are at a loss, sacrificing him as he beseeches. But he, not hearing his cries, kills him and concerns himself with an evil feast in his house. In just the same way son takes father and children

5   their mother (5), and bereaving them of life eat their dear flesh.

Fr. 6

For first hear that there are four roots of all things: bright Zeus and Hera bearer of life and Aidoneus and Nestis who moistens mortal springs with her tears.

Fr. 17

I shall tell a two-fold story. For at one time things grew from several to be one alone, at another time they grew apart to be several from one. There is a double birth of mortal things and a double destruction: for the coming together of everything creates and destroys the one, while the

5   other having been nurtured flies apart again when things are growing apart (5). And things never cease continuously changing, at one time through Love everything coming together into one, and at another time each thing being borne apart through the hatred of Strife. Thus in which respect they have learnt to grow into one from many and again spring as

10   many from one as it grows apart again (10), in that respect they are in a state of becoming and there is no lasting time for them; but in which respect they never cease continually changing, in *that* respect they are always unchanging in a cycle.

But come, listen to my words; for learning improves the mind. For as

15   I said earlier too, uttering the results of my words (15), I shall tell a double story. For at one time they grew to be one alone from several, and at another time they grew apart to be several from one, fire and water and earth and the boundless height of air, and destructive Strife apart from them, in equal amount everywhere, and Love among them,

20   equal in length and breadth (20). Her you look at with your mind, do not sit astonished with your eyes. She is regarded as inborn in mortal limbs, and through her they think friendly thoughts and do harmonious deeds, calling her by name Joy and Aphrodite. Her no mortal man has perceived as she whirls among these (25), but you listen to the

25   undeceitful voyage of my tale. For these elements are all equal and of the

same age by birth, but each controls a different prerogative and each has its own nature. And they hold sway in turn in the course of the passage of time. And in addition to them not a thing arises or ceases (30). For if they were being utterly destroyed, they would no longer now exist. And **30** what would increase this whole, and coming from where? And in what way could they even utterly perish, since there is nothing devoid of these? But just these things exist, and running through each other they become different things at different times and are continuously always alike (35).

Fr. 29

For from its back two branches do not shoot out, nor feet, nor swift knees nor creative genitals, but it was a sphere and equal to itself from every direction.

Fr. 28

But it is equal to itself from all directions and everywhere boundless, a rounded sphere rejoicing in its surrounding solitude.

Fr. 30

But when Strife had grown great in respect of its limbs and leapt up into honours in the fulfilment of time which, coming as an exchange for them, has been drawn up by a broad oath ...

Fr. 31

For all the limbs of the god began to shake one after the other.

Fr. 134

For it is not adorned in its limbs with a mortal head, nor from its back do two branches shoot out, nor feet, nor swift knees, nor hairy genitals, but it is simply ineffable, holy mind, darting over the whole universe with swift thoughts.

Fr. 115

These lines almost certainly come from the beginning of Empedocles' philosophical poem *On Nature*; some of them are quoted by Plutarch, with the comment, 'Empedocles, having made the introductory announcement at the beginning of his philosophy ...'. Traditionally, despite what Plutarch says, they have been placed after Empedocles' physical account of the world, at the start of what was believed to be a second and separate poem, *Purifications*, but the recent papyrus discovery tends to support Plutarch and suggests they formed the start of a single work (although Plutarch's 'at the beginning' need not necessarily mean 'at the very beginning', and it is possible to suppose that Fr. 112, where Empedocles seems to be introducing himself, was the start of the whole poem).

The lines reveal Empedocles' personal belief in the Pythagorean belief in reincarnation and link it with the four elements of his physics: to expiate a misdemeanour his soul has fallen and must wander 30,000 years (or 10,000 years, if one assumes a three-season year and that 'season' here means 'season' and not 'year') through a cycle of reincarnations. The misdemeanour is not specified, but is probably blood sacrifice of an animal, contrary to the strict vegetarianism that many Pythagoreans practised, but the text is uncertain at the crucial point (**2** 'pollutes'). Empedocles appears to link this Pythagorean soul-doctrine with his physics, where (as described more fully in the introduction above) he posits a cosmic cycle dominated by alternating forces of Love and Strife which alternately unite and fragment the four elements, air, fire, earth, water: as our soul (fallen from the state of Love) becomes increasingly corrupted by Strife, it is tossed about by the four elements until Strife wanes, Love returns and, 30,000 years (?) later, the soul is perfect, divine love again. The lines tell us that at one time Empedocles was living a blessed, godly existence, but now Strife has caused him to be alienated from god.

1 *Necessity*: the Presocratics regularly attribute to Necessity ultimate causes for which they can give no further explanation; cf. Heraclitus B 80.

2–4 *whenever one ... whoever ... one of the gods*: i.e. 'whenever one of the gods who have obtained a share of blessed life pollutes (?) his own limbs ... or commits a sin in strife (?) ...'.

2–3 *pollutes his own limbs with the blood of slaughter*: 'pollutes' is an uncertain reading, but cf. Frr. 128, 136, 137, 139 where Empedocles cries out against slaughter and sacrifice. One problem is how blood-sacrifice could have been the original sin, as when the soul was a god and combined with perfect Love, *i.e.* part of the divine sphere, it was presumably non-corporeal and lacked limbs (cf. M-P 62). A solution is to suppose that Empedocles refers here to a time when the sphere of Love has not yet been reached in the cosmic cycle.

4 *swears a false oath*: swearing a false oath starts the soul's decline, but a lacuna in the Greek text – 'in strife' is a modern editorial supplement – means that again details are unclear.

4–5 *one of the gods ... blessed life*: the implication is that before the start of the fall, the soul was in a blessed state, *i.e.* living harmoniously as part of the world under the sway of total Love.

7–10 *For the strength of the air ... eddies of the sky*: the fallen soul or spirit is cast from one of the four elements to another, not allowed to settle but forced by Strife to wander through a cycle of reincarnation.

12 *mad strife*: Strife disrupts on the personal level as well as on the cosmic level. On the personal level it equates to participation in sacrifice (cf. Fr. 139 below).

Fr. 117

The various forms of life that Empedocles has been in his previous reincarnations.

Fr. 112

Empedocles now represents himself as an immortal god, promoting benefits for his home city. It is not clear how, if at all, he attempted to fit his divinity here into the theory of his physics: it should imply that he lives in a state of cosmic harmony under the sway of Love, his soul harmoniously reinstated into the mass of divine love and knowledge (cf. Fr. 134) – but see general introduction above (last sentence); or perhaps he is one of the souls which are having their last life on earth before being released from the cycle of reincarnations altogether (see Sharples on Plato, *Meno* 81c 1–4 with references).

2 Acragas in Sicily was a centre of Pythagoreanism. Pindar's *Olympian* 2, praising a victory in the chariot race by Theron, tyrant of Acragas, also contains an account of the soul's fate, ending with how the souls of good people have a blessed life among the gods. (*O.* 2.56–77).

4 *as an immortal god*: see introduction to this fragment.

5 Empedocles' elevated status is like that of an athletics victor.

5–9 He is sought after as a seer or doctor, traditionally wise men.

Frr. 127, 146, 147

We go through a heirarchy of lives when Love is on the ascendency, starting off as beings almost totally separate from divine bliss when Strife is dominant, ending up as gods. In 127 and 146 Empedocles lists the best types of life at various stages. Lions are the top-ranked animals; bay the best plant; seers, poets, doctors and leaders (= kings) the best people.

Fr. 127

1 *they become*: the subject is 'mortals when reincarnated at the highest level during the animal stage of the cycle of reincarnation'.

Fr. 146

2 A reminder of 'the status of gods as beings not totally different from men but as having the same origin and constitution as them', Wright. In Empedocles' view, gods 'grow up' as part of a universal physical process as much as any other being.

Fr. 147

The life of the blessed when they have reached divine status. All divine beings are together and a harmonious unity, just as the world under Love is on a cosmic scale; in contrast, under Strife, the universe is fragmented and mortal spirits are far away from the divine. (115.9).

1 *sharing a hearth with the other immortals, being at the same table*: in more conventional mythology mortals and immortals lived together and shared the same table during the Golden Age; cf. *Hesiodic Catalogue of Women* Fr. 1.6–7, Virgil *Eclogue* 4.15–16.

Frr. 130, 135, 139, 136, 137

The fall from Love and harmony caused by the sin of bloodshed and sacrifice.

Fr. 130

All living things are akin and, when Love is dominant, united by Friendship. This kinship explains how, when the break-up appears, mortals can change into living things of a different order.

Fr. 135

Quoted by Aristotle (*Rhet.* 1373b) to illustrate the universality of law: ' ... as Empedocles says about not killing living beings; for this law is not just for some while unjust for others'.

Fr. 139

This fragment implies, in the light of Frr. 130 and 135, that meat-eating is a sin. The new papyrus gives fragments of four lines before these; the immediately preceding one (d4) probably mentions the Harpies, vicious birds of prey, (the line as restored saying that the Harpies will soon be with us), giving some support to the version of the line printed here, with 'claws' of the papyrus, against the traditional version, deriving from Porphyry's quotation, with 'lips' (see Martin-Primavesi 297–302, 344–5).

Bob Sharples adds: 'If there's a connection between the Harpies' claws and those in fr. 139, it is, I think, going to have to be something like 'those who eat meat like Harpies, and so with metaphorical claws, will necessarily find themselves among/torn apart by real Harpies.' Perhaps that's not too strange for Empedocles (!); but I note that lions (Fr. 127) too have claws, and that if the reference were to them the implication would be that humans eating animals is in principle no different from one non-human animal preying on another'.

Fr. 136

The emphasis is on 'one another': 'Don't you see that it's *one another* that you are devouring ...' (sc. perhaps 'when you eat sacrificial victims, given that all living things are akin').

Fr. 137

Empedocles horrifically represents a man performing an animal sacrifice as (since all living things are akin) performing an act tantamount to the slaying of his own son, and likewise with sacrifices performed by other members of the family. Strife, though not explicitly mentioned, is clearly a causal factor.

1 The sacrificial animal is in fact the father's reincarnated son.
2–3 *And they are at a loss ... But he, not hearing his cries*: text uncertain; 'at a loss' and 'not hearing' are conjectures by Diels.

Fr. 6

We now turn to Empedocles' physics. Here he says that the four basic elements ('roots') which make up all things are gods, although there is (and was even in antiquity) dispute as to which elements are represented by the first three gods. Nestis is explained by Empedocles as water. The epithet 'bright' of Zeus suggests he is fire, as one would expect from his traditional lightning and thunderbolt. Aidoneus is a lengthened, poetic form of Aides = Hades = Underworld, suggesting he stands for Earth – which leaves Hera as Air (see Wright pp. 165–166).

In naming the elements as gods Empedocles is radically re-casting the roles of the traditional gods of mythology: gods exist, but as physical substances in the world. The divine permeates the physical world. The start of this approach to philosophy and religion can be found already in the enigmatic dictum attributed to Thales, the first Greek philosopher, 'Everything is full of gods'. Both Empedocles and Thales believe in a type of pantheism.

1 *For*: we do not know what preceded this fragment in Empedocles' poem.
first: these lines evidently opened his account of the physical world.
hear: his addressee is, formally, Pausanias, son of Anchites (mentioned in Fr. 1), about whom nothing is known.
2 *Nestis*: possibly a Sicilian name for Persephone, equated with water because of the tears she shed when forced to live half the year underground.

Fr. 17

This fragment, the longest surviving one (and the papyrus discovery extends it further, beyond what is given here), explains the means by which the four elements combine and separate: it is due to the workings of two divine forces, Love and Strife. So here, again, Empedocles radically changes traditional ideas about the nature of the gods. Love (Aphrodite) was an Olympian goddess. Strife, though involved with mythology to a much lesser extent, is a goddess in Homer (*Il.* 11.10) and Hesiod (*Theog.* 224ff. where she is a daughter of Night). Love and Strife, alternating in their ascendency, produce Empedocles' famous cosmic cycle. As Love predominates, and Strife decreases, the elements cause things in the world to become more and more unified until the universe is nothing but a single god in the form of a rounded sphere. At this time Strife is eradicated, but then it comes into being again, increases, causes the sphere to disrupt and separates things more and more until everything is separated into minimal units. At this time Love is eradicated, but then it too increases, and eventually we are back to the sphere. Things can be created both during the ascendency of Love and during the ascendency of Strife, but it is unclear over what time-span Love and Strife operate and in what type of era we are now living (one of increasing Love or one of increasing Strife).

The new papyrus continues Fr. 17 with fragments of 33 lines. On one occasion (c3, corresponding to Fr. 20.2 Diels-Kranz), and as an alternative on another occasion (a(i)6; cf. also a(ii)17), the papyrus says '*we* come together', not 'the elements/things come together'. This use of 'we' could indicate Empedocles wanting to combine his physics and his demonology (cf. Martin-Primavesi 90–95, 346–347); but against reading too much into this use of 'we', see Osborne 344–352.

3 *There is a double birth of mortal things and a double destruction*: things can come into being, or be destroyed, both when Love is in the ascendency and when Strife is.

3–4 *the coming together of everything*: when Love is effective.

5–6 *when things are growing apart*: when Strife is effective. The text is uncertain, but the idea is that under increasing Strife there is a process of creation but the general tendency is towards separation. It seems from Aristotle (*DA* 2.4 415b28) that Empedocles explained plants as the (temporary) products of fire on its way up (as a result of Strife separating out the elements) meeting earth on its way down.

15 *the results of my words*: *i.e.* my message.

16–17 The repetition (of **1–2**) is characteristic of epic, the genre to which Empedocles is indebted for many aspects of his style.

18 *destructive Strife*: Strife has (unless 'destructive' is just a conventional epithet) pejorative connotations even in the physical world, an additional reason for believing that Empedocles tried to harmonise his ethics with his physics (see introduction to fr. 17).

19–20 *in equal amount ... equal in length and breadth*: Strife and Love are equal, uniform, inasmuch as they affect all the elements equally.

23 *Joy and Aphrodite*: so the cosmic force Love is, in Empedocles' view, the same as the love that mortals experience and the goddess Aphrodite: the divine permeates the world.

28 *a thing*: this seems required by the sense, but can only be accommodated by means of a very dubious elision in the Greek.

28–34 *For if they were being utterly destroyed ... are continuously always alike*: the roots/elements are immortal and ubiquitous.

28–32 Empedocles applies to his roots reasoning used by Parmenides on the nature of reality (Fr. 8.6–7, 19–20, 23–5, 44–8).

31–2 *since there is nothing devoid of these*: *i.e.* the roots are everywhere.

Frr. 29 and 28
The nature of maximal Love. Love is a god (see Fr. 31) in the form of a sphere. Empedocles' dscription comes form Parmenides' description of the nature of reality (Fr. 8.29–31). Strictly speaking, it is the elements conglomerated by Love that are spherical, rather than Love itself, but Empedocles conceives of the bonding force of Love as itself spherical.

29.1 Love has no arms.

Frr. 30–31
The growth of Strife and waning, and destruction, of Love.

Fr. 30
3 *them*: the roots.

Fr. 31
And so the god Love fragments.

limbs: metaphorical in the sense of 'stretches', 'areas'.
of the god: 'important as the only identification in the fragment of the sphere with a god' (Wright 192).
began to shake: the Greek expression is used by Homer (*Il.* 8.443) of Mt. Olympus quaking under the feet of Zeus, so reinforcing here the divine nature of Strife.

Fr. 134
Empedocles extended his rebuttal of traditional views of the gods by classing mind, too, as divine. Here his description of mind repeats his description of the perfect harmony of the elements under Love, perhaps implying that for Empedocles thought is identical with a harmonious blend of the elements, and that if man uses pure mind, divorcing himself from erroneous beliefs, he is tantamount to a god (cf. Fr. 112.4).

3–4 *darting over the whole universe with swift thoughts*: in one's thoughts one can range over the entire universe without interference, as do all the elements under Love; mind, therefore, is analogous to the world under the sway of Love.

8. Plato *Symposium* 209e5–212a7: Divine Forms

This passage is the culmination of Socrates' speech in Plato's *Symposium*. In it Socrates reports what he was told about love by Diotima, a Mantinean priestess. All the speeches of the *Symposium* are related by a character, Apollodorus, on the basis of what he heard from a first-hand witness, Aristodemus. So Diotima's account reaches us, the readers, fourth-hand. The purpose of this narrative presentation is unclear, but it has the effect of distancing us from what is said, thereby inviting us to question it – which is just the effect Socrates thought philosophical probing ought to have.

Diotima here encourages us to revise our traditional views on the nature of love: love is not merely physical, but has a more important spiritual and philosophical dimension; at the highest level it represents a desire to seek a vision of the Form of Beauty, an eternal and divine entity which Plato thought was responsible for all the secondary examples of beauty seen in material objects. Someone who grasps this wondrous object with his mind's eye himself becomes, as far as is possible for a human being, divine and immortal, because he will have grasped something more permanent, more divine, than anything in our messy world.

Diotima does not dismiss physical love, but urges us to use it as a mere stepping-stone to this higher love. It is not clear exactly what the 'grasping' involves, but the language used of it suggests it comes in an exalted vision, and this is supported by her comparison between her protreptic and the Higher Mysteries at Eleusis where the initiate in a moment of revelation underwent an emotional and spiritual transformation, glimpsing god and learning to move from the earthly and physical to the divine, by replacing fear of death with contentment, in the knowledge that confrontation with death would be a happy experience.

The whole speech is bizarre, and in a number of places the arguments are thin and questionable. In particular, the thesis at the heart of the speech that true love is a desire for immortality is based on a number of very flimsy inferences and analogies. But, as with many Platonic *mythoi*, fictional stories containing a kernel of profound insight, the purpose of the narrative form is to persuade not so much through logic as through emotional appeal.

The Forms appear in a number of Platonic dialogues. They are unchanging, divine entities that do not belong to this world. Plato uses them to persuade us of his idea that truth and reality are not relative to individuals in this world, but belong to another realm altogether, a divine world. If we can come to see the Forms, we can make contact with the divine and bridge the gulf between man and god. The Forms themselves are a Platonic invention, perhaps in his view implicit in the discussions of his teacher Socrates; but the idea that understanding the truth involves a vision of the divine, a vision of something transcending anything in this world, can be traced back in its most explicit form to the Way of Truth of Parmenides, a generation earlier than Socrates, where what exists is perfect, unchanging and revealed to him by a goddess (Frr. 1, 8); there are antecedents, too, in the sixth-century philosopher Xenophanes' picture of god: according to Xenophanes, what exists, the universe, is god who is unchanging and perfect (Frr. 25, 26 with Simplicius' commentary). In addition, the idea that the nature of the mind interacts with its object ('like perceives like'), so that if something divine is grasped there must be something divine in us that is grasping it, can be traced back to earlier theories of perception (cf. Empedocles Fr. 109, 'By earth we see earth ...').

Diotima's speech to Socrates actually begins before the passage commented on below. Love is an intermediary between human and divine worlds, she says, enabling humans to contact the divine (202e3–4). Specifically, love is a force which impels us to seek to acquire a philosophical attitude (204b2–4). This impulse or desire is for a type of immortality, because (says Diotima) everyone wishes *always* to possess good things (205a6–7, 206a9–12). This idea that we truly desire only what is good is central to Plato's philosophy, and sometimes referred to as 'the sovereignty of the good'. How precisely does one achieve this type of immortality? Through begetting 'in the beautiful' says Diotima: all people desire sex, to reproduce; reproduction is a perpetuation of oneself; therefore, we all desire to create a type of immortality for ourselves (206c5–8, 206e8–207a4). The reasoning, here as elsewhere in Diotima's speech, is questionable, of course, as a desire for something always to be available to one is not necessarily the same as a desire for immortality ('always' is vague, meaning both 'for all time' and merely 'for as long as one lives'). But Diotima continues by saying that the desire she is talking about is a natural process, not only physically through its creation of offspring, but spiritually through renewing our thoughts, emotion and knowledge; those who are especially fertile spiritually or in their soul, give birth to virtue and wisdom, having a share in 'children' (their 'works') that are more attractive and immortal than ordinary children (209c6–7). This brings us to the passage that follows. For a clear summary of 204d1–209e4, pointing out the oddity of some of the arguments, see Rowe 177–178, and for a reading of the whole passage below see Rowe 192–3.

Bibliography

Plato, *Symposium* ed. K. J. Dover (Cambridge 1980).
J. Annas, *An Introduction to Plato's Republic* (Oxford 1981) 205–6, 217–241.
Plato *Symposium* ed. C. Rowe (Warminster 1998).

'Even you might perhaps be initiated into these matters of love, Socrates, but I do not know if you would be able to be initiated into the rites and final secrets which are the goal of that teaching (210), if one pursues it properly. I shall speak,' she said, 'and shall not be wanting in eagerness,
5 and you try to follow if you can. For it is necessary,' she said, 'for the person who is entering upon this pursuit to begin, when he is young, to go towards beautiful bodies, and first, if the person guiding him is guiding him properly, for him to love one body and there engender

beautiful words, and then for him to realise that beauty in any one body
10   is a brother to love for any other body (210b), and if it is necessary to
pursue love of physical form it is great folly for him not to believe that
beauty with respect to all bodies is one and the same; and realising this,
it is necessary for him to become a lover of all beautiful bodies, and
to relax his very great passion for just one, despising it and thinking
15   it petty; and after this he should think beauty in the soul more valuable
than that in the body, so that even if someone good with respect to his
soul should have only a small attraction, it is necessary for this to be
sufficient for him to love and care for, and for him to produce and seek
fine words (210c) of the sort that will make the young better, so that he
20   might be compelled to look again at beauty in activities and laws and see
this, that it is all akin to itself, in order that he might believe that physical
beauty is petty; after activities he should lead him towards the varieties
of knowledge, so that he can now see the beauty of knowing things, and,
looking now at a wealth of beauty, so that he is no longer a cheap and
25   petty person loving like a slave (210d) in servitude the beauty residing
in a single body of a boy or of a person or of a single activity, but so
that, turned towards the great sea of beauty and contemplating it, he
might beget much beautiful and magnificent discussion and thoughts in
unstinting philosophy, until strengthened and invigorated there he views
30   a single type of knowledge which is of this sort of beauty.

Try to pay attention to me,' she said, 'as much as possible (210e).
For whoever has been educated with regard to love up to this point,
seeing beautiful things correctly and in succession, now going towards
the culmination of love he will suddenly catch sight of a beauty of
35   wondrous nature, this one, Socrates, for the sake of which all the
previous exertions were, firstly always existing and neither coming into
existence nor perishing, nor increasing (211) nor decaying, secondly not
a beauty that is beautiful in one respect but ugly in another respect, nor
one that is beautiful at one time but not at another time, nor beautiful
40   with reference to one thing but ugly with reference to another, nor
beautiful here but ugly there, being beautiful to some people but ugly to
others; nor again will the beauty be presented to him as a face or hands
or anything else which the body has a share in, nor as an argument or
a piece of knowledge, nor as being somewhere in something else, such
45   as in an animal or earth or heaven or in anything else; but it is always
existing, of single form (211b), itself by itself with itself, with all the

other beautiful things partaking in it in this sort of way, such that, while the other beautiful things are coming to be and perishing, that one is not becoming more or less at all and is not affected in any way at all.

50   'When someone, ascending from these starting-points through the correct love of boys, begins to see that beauty, he would almost be in touch with the goal. For this is the right way to go, or to be led by someone else, towards love, namely starting (211c) from the beautiful objects here in this world always to ascend for the sake of that beauty,

55   using the former like stepping-stones: from one to two, and from two to all beautiful bodies, and from beautiful bodies to beautiful activities, and from activities to beautiful intellectual pursuits, and from intellectual pursuits to end up ascending to that intellectual pursuit which is the intellectual pursuit of nothing other than that Form of Beauty, and finally

60   actually to recognise the Form of Beauty. 'At that point in one's life, my dear Socrates,' said (211d) the lady stranger from Mantinea, 'if anywhere else, life for a human being is worth living, as he sees the Form of Beauty. If you ever see it, it will not seem to you like gold or clothes or beautiful boys and young men at the sight of whom now you

65   are smitten and are ready, both you and many other men who see boys and are always with them, if it were somehow possible, neither to eat or drink but just gaze and be with them. What, then,' she said, 'do we think if it happened to someone that he saw the Form of Beauty, absolute, pure, unmixed (211e) and not full of mortal flesh and colours

70   and a lot of other mortal rubbish, but to see the unique, divine Form of Beauty? Do you think,' she said, 'that the life of a person looking at it is insignificant, or that the part of him with which it is necessary for him to look (212a), as he sees it and is with it, is insignificant? Or do you not realise,' she said, 'that it will happen to him there alone, if he is seeing

75   Beauty with the part by which it must be seen, to beget not images of goodness, since he is not in contact with an image, but truth, since he is in contact with the truth. And since he is begetting and nurturing true goodness, it is possible for him to become dear to the gods, and, if for any other person, for that person too to become immortal.'

1–4 *Even you might perhaps be initiated... if one pursues it properly*: Plato compares what is to follow in Diotima's speech with the experience of being initiated into a mystery cult. The analogy is appropriate because mystical initiation (a) was in two parts the first of which was a pre-condition for the second, just as Socrates' understanding of what Diotima has said so far is a pre-condition for his understanding what follows, and (b) offered the initiate an encounter with the divine, with happiness replacing fear of death, by means of a vision, just as Plato is offering a vision of immortality. On mystery-cult initiation, see W.Burkert, *Ancient Mystery Cults* (Cambridge MA and London 1987), *Homo Necans* (English translation: Berkeley 1983), 248–297, esp. 274–297.

5–30 A long sentence ('perhaps meant to be recalling some list of ritual instructions', Rowe on 210a4–5) describing the stepping-stones to Platonic love.

7–8 *if the person guiding him is guiding him properly*: love requires two males, as Plato models it loosely on the typically Greek homosexual relationship (older lover ~ younger beloved); in the mysteries, too, a *mystagogos* guided would-be-initiates (see Rowe ad loc.)

19–20 *so that he might be compelled to look again at beauty*: the idea that the lover should be 'compelled' towards Platonic love may seem repugnant, but both here where Plato is trying to reform people's attitude to love, and in the *Republic* where more wholescale educational reforms are outlined (see 'Compulsion in the state' in the index to Annas' book mentioned in the Bibliography above), compulsion is a key means to reform.

27–30 *turned towards the great sea of beauty ... this sort of beauty*: the final stage of love comes from philosophy: it is a vision of boundless beauty that enables one to 'see' a unique knowledge (of the divine Form of Beauty). Note the frequent use of 'seeing' verbs to describe how one gets this understanding of true beauty (cf. 'seeing' 33, 'catch sight of' 34, 'see' 51): it comes through a type of mystical and spiritual vision (see Annas, 238). The Forms – objective reality – underpin a number of Platonic dialogues. For an excellent discussion of them, see Annas ch.9.

28 *beautiful and magnificent discussion*: the medium philosophy uses to generate the ultimate vision, just as on the physical level love between beautiful bodies generates children.

34–49 The unchanging, divine Form of Beauty, which stays the same and is not relative to the individual.

46–9 *with all the other beautiful things ... not affected in any way at all*: particular beautiful things somehow get their beauty from the Form of Beauty; they eventually die, but it remains everlasting.

50–60 Plato recapitulates the stepping-stones to the vision of the Form of Beauty.

70 The Form of Beauty is divine.

74–5 *seeing Beauty with the part by which it must be seen*: contemplation of the Form of Beauty is done by a special part of the soul (reason/intelligence).

77–9 *And since ... immortal*: in the contemplation of something divine and immortal, one becomes divine and immortal – as far as is possible for a human being. The idea that 'Like sees like' is common in Greek philosophy.

9. Aristotle *Nicomachean Ethics* 1177b26–1179a23: Divine *theoria*

Aristotle has shown that perfect happiness consists in contemplation (*theoria*); he now goes on to show its divine nature. Although most of the preceding chapters of the *Nicomachean Ethics* had concentrated on moral virtue as the source of human happiness, he had always left open the possibility that a certain type of intellectual virtue could bring a higher, divine, form of happiness (cf. 1098a16–18 'The good for man is an activity of soul in accordance with virtue, and if there are several virtues in accordance with the best and most perfect'; 1102a3–4 'the first principle and cause of good things we reckon to be valuable and divine'). But given that Aristotle thought that only the intellect in man is divine, and man is a composite being composed of intellect and body, a man cannot live on a divine plane all the time. Therefore, although Aristotle believes that contemplation alone gives perfect happiness, because the contemplator is a human being and lives in a community, he will also perform acts of virtue and gain from them a second-rate happiness.

But what does the contemplator contemplate, and how does he do it? In Aristotle's other ethical work, the *Eudemian Ethics*, contemplation is spelt out as contemplation of god (*EE* 1249b 6–21), but here in the *NE* Aristotle is less precise. Yet he gives some clues: contemplators are wise people (1177a34, 1179a32), so they are exercisers of wisdom or *sophia*. In Bk. 6 of the *NE* he had more to say about wisdom: the wise man intuits first principles (with intelligence or *nous*) and knows what follows from them (using understanding or *episteme*). What this in practice means is that the contemplator contemplates truths about the world and the knowledge he possesses about what can be deduced from them (cf. Kenny 104: 'It is knowledge coupled with the intelligence to see how individual items of knowledge fit together within the whole systematic context within which they are embedded').

This use of *nous* is one reason why contemplation is a divine activity: in Aristotle's view, *nous* enters a person's body from outside and is independent of the body; *nous* is an intelligence inherent in the world, something impersonal. Since *nous* is not human (and certainly not a feature of animals, *NE* 1178b25–6), and since the exercise of *nous* while contemplating is a divine activity (it is the sole activity of god, *NE* 1178b6–24), *nous* must be divine. But this means that contemplation itself is a divine activity in two ways: it uses a divine part of us, and its objects (*i.e.* what we think of when we think with *nous*) are divine. The second way is so because when we use our *nous* the thoughts we think of are created by our *nous*.

The above is a brief interpretation of a difficult subject. Aristotle makes some questionable assumptions that he does not argue for (*e.g.* that *nous* is divine), and some of his arguments are not compelling (*e.g.* that the sole activity of god is contemplation). The result is a protreptic to philosophy that will perhaps appeal to philosophers (like Aristotle), but be less attractive to others. One can compare the central sections of Plato's *Republic* where Plato has recourse to some famous flights of imagination and emotional persuasion (especially in the Sun, Line and Cave similies) to promote the study of philosophy.

Bibliography

S. J. Clark, *Aristotle's Man* (Oxford 1975) 157–163.
J. O. Urmson, *Aristotle's Ethics* (Oxford 1988) 118–127.
A. J. P. Kenny, *Aristotle and the Perfect Life* (Oxford 1992) 86–112.

But such a life would be more than human; for a person will not live it like this as a human but as there exists something divine in him. And as much as this divine part differs from the composite person, so much does its activity differ from that according to the other virtue. If the intellect is
5   divine in comparison with a human being, so too also is a life lived in accordance with the intellect compared with human life. One must not live according to those who urge one to think human thoughts since one is a human, or mortal thoughts since one is mortal, but it is necessary to be immortal as much as is possible and to do everything towards
10   living according to the best part in one. For even if in terms of (1178a) size it is small, in terms of power and value it far exceeds everything. And each person would seem to be this, since it is the ruling and better part. For it would be absurd if someone were to choose not the life belonging to himself but that belonging to
15   something else. And what was said before will apply now too.
    For what belongs to each person is naturally best and most pleasant for each person. And for a human, life lived according to the intellect, since this [*i.e.* intellect] is what a human being most of all is, will also be the happiest type of life.
20   Life lived in accordance with the other virtue has a second-rate happiness. For activities in accordance with it are merely human. For in our activities with each other we do just deeds and brave deeds and so on in accordance with the virtues, in our dealings and business

transactions and all types of action and experience, maintaining what is
25 right for each of us. All these seem to belong to humans. Some seem to
arise from the body, and moral virtue seems to exist to a large extent in
combination with feelings. Prudence is joined with moral virtue, and
moral virtue with prudence, if the starting-points for prudence are with
the moral virtues, and correctness in the moral virtues is achieved with
30 prudence. They are joined with the feelings and would be concerned
with the composite person; and the virtues of the composite are human;
and so is the life lived according to them and the happiness. But the
happiness of the intellect is separate. For let so much be said about it, for
to go into the matter in detail is beyond the scope of the present inquiry.
35 It would seem to need outside support to a small degree or to a lesser
degree than moral virtue. Let it be admitted there is for both an equal
need for necessities, even if someone living a political life labours with
more concern for the body and so on; for in this respect there would
be little difference. But in terms of their activities there will be a huge
40 difference. For the liberal man will need money for doing liberal acts,
and the just man for giving back what he owes (for intentions reveal
nothing: even unjust people pretend to want to do just acts), and the
brave man will need ability, if he is to accomplish anything virtuously,
and the self-controlled man opportunity. For how otherwise will he or
45 any of the others be conspicuous? It is disputed whether choice or
deeds are more important for virtue, since it is related to both (1178b).
But it is clear that perfect virtue would be located in both. There is need
of many things for deeds, and the greater and finer the deeds the more
things are needed. But for the man who contemplates there is no need
50 for such things for the actualisation of his activity, but one might say
they are even an impediment to contemplation. But inasmuch as he is a
human being and lives with a number of people, he will choose to act
virtuously; so he will need such things to be a human being.

That perfect happiness is a contemplative activity would seem to
55 follow from this. For we have assumed that the gods are especially
blessed and happy. But what actions is it necessary to assign to them?
Just ones? But they will seem ridiculous entering into contracts and
returning deposits and doing all that sort of thing. Brave ones? But they
will seem equally ridiculous enduring fearful situations and taking risks
60 for what is good. Liberal ones? To whom shall they give? It will be
absurd if they shall have money or suchlike. And what would be self-

controlled deeds for them? To praise them for being self-controlled would be vulgar, since they do not have bad desires. In everything they do anything concerned with normal activities would appear trivial and
65 unworthy of the gods. And yet everyone has assumed they live and are active – for they do not sleep like Endymion. If we take away from that whch is alive doing things, and even more so making things, what is left except contemplation? So the activity of god, distinguished by its blessedness, would be contemplative. And of human activities the
70 one closest to this would be happiest. Proof of this is the fact that other animals do not partake in happiness, since they are completely deprived of such activity. For the gods all their life is blessed, for humans to the extent that there exists some similarity in activity. No other living thing is happy, since in no way does it partake in contemplation. As far
75 as contemplation extends, so too happiness, and the more contemplation someone has the more happiness – not coincidentally, but through contemplation. For it is valued in itself. So happiness would be some form of contemplation. But for a human there will be need too of outside good fortune, for human nature is not self-sufficient for contemplation,
80 but the body needs to be healthy, and there must be a supply of food and other care. But one must not think that to be happy there will be need of many large things, (1179a) just because it is not possible to be blessed without some external goods. For self-sufficiency does not require an excess, nor does action, but even someone who does not
85 rule earth and sea can do fine deeds. For even from moderate resources someone could act virtuously (This is clear to see: for private citizens do not seem to do fine deeds less than people in official positions but even more so). It is sufficient if such resources exist. For the life of a person acting virtuously will be happy. And Solon perhaps defined
90 happy people well, saying they were moderately equipped with external resources, doing the finest deeds, in his opinion, and living sensibly. For it is possible for those with moderate resources to do what is necessary. Anaxagoras too seems to have assumed that the happy person was not a wealthy or powerful one, saying that he would not be surprised if the
95 happy person should seem odd to the majority. For they judge by externals, taking notice of them alone.

So the opinions of the wise seem to agree with this account. Therefore, such a view has credibility. But the truth in matters of action is judged from deeds and one's life; for in these areas lies the critical

factor. So, to examine the aforesaid one must take into account deeds
100 and life, and accept what agrees with the account and assume only
provisionally what disagrees. And the person active with his mind, and
caring for this, seems to be in the best condition and most loved by the
gods.

2 *something divine*: intelligence.
3 *the composite person*: consisting of body and soul, *i.e.* having both divine
intelligence and non-divine body.
4 *the other virtue*: moral virtue. Just as the intellect by itself is superior to man
regarded as intellect + body, so the excellent activity of the intellect by itself (*i.e.*
contemplation) surpasses that of composite man (*i.e.* moral virtue). The next
sentence clarifies this point of view.
6–10 *One must not ... the best part in one*: Aristotle is being quite radical here, in
advising that we try to cross the boundary that divides us from god. By 'those who
urge' he has in mind *e.g.* Pindar *Isthmian* 5.20 'mortal things are appropriate for
mortals'.
8–9 *it is necessary to be immortal*: or 'to participate in immortality'. 'En contemplant,
nous imitons pour court instant l'activité éternelle de Dieu' (Gauthier-Jolif ad loc.).
10–11 *in terms of size it is small*: in Aristotle's view *nous* is immaterial, so in fact
has no bulk at all.
12–15 *And each person ... something else*: If the intellect is the highest part of us,
then we are intellect and our true life is a life of intellectual activity.
16 *what was said before*: cf. 1099a21 'If this is so, actions done in accordance with
virtue would be intrinsically pleasant'; 1170a14–16 'For it has been said that what
is good by nature is good for the good man and is intrinsically pleasant'. Aristotle
thinks that activity in conformity with virtue is essentially pleasant, and that the
activity in conformity with the highest (intellectual) virtue (viz. contemplation,
which essentially belongs to man) will essentially be most pleasant.
20–1 *Life lived in accordance with the other virtue has a second-rate happiness*:
a life devoted only to moral virtue, without contemplation, is a second-rate life,
because it does not use the divine element in us.
24–5 *maintaining what is right for each of us*: referring to the Doctrine of the Mean
(cf. esp. *NE* 2.6), Aristotle's theory that for moral virtue one must avoid extremes
in actions and feelings and be guided by a sense of what is appropriate to particular
circumstances.
25–6 *Some seem to arise from the body*: Aristotle thought some feelings are
essentially bodily reactions, *e.g.* blushing (1128b14–15).
26–32 *moral virtue seems to exist to a large extent in combination with feelings ...
and so is the life lived according to them and the happiness*: moral virtue involves
bodily feelings; it also has an intellectual aspect (prudence, *phronesis*), but even

this (unlike contemplation) is linked to the practical side of man, since prudence considers what one ought to do (1140b21–2: 'prudence is a true state accompanied by reason involving action concerning what is good for human beings').

30–1 *They are joined with the feelings ... composite person*: the principles used by prudence, being linked to our feelings, relate to the composite side of man.

35–6 *It would seem to need outside support ... to a lesser degree than moral virtue*: Aristotle goes on (**49–51**) to say why contemplation is a largely self-sufficient activity, repeating what he said earlier (10.4–5).

36 *both*: the happiness of moral virtue and the happiness of contemplation.

40–9 Practitioners of moral virtue need external goods, so that they have the opportunity of displaying their virtues – otherwise we shall never know that they really are virtuous.

45 *choice*: a moral virtue requires actions that are chosen by the agent.

51–3 *But inasmuch as he is a human being ... he will need such things to be a human being*: the contemplator is a human being, a 'political animal', so, however much he contemplates, inasmuch as he lives in a *polis* he will also choose to act virtuously.

54 *perfect happiness is a contemplative activity*: contemplation by itself provides a happiness that is complete, without the need for other purveyors of lesser happiness such as wealth or pleasure or moral virtue. See further, Kenny 16–22.

54–69 Further arguments aimed to show that perfect happiness is contemplation. Firstly, god contemplates, so if we are to be god-like we too should contemplate; secondly, animals cannot contemplate, so contemplation must be a higher form of activity.

66 *Endymion*: loved by the moon he retained his beauty for ever, but in an eternal sleep.

74–8 *As far as contemplation extends ... some form of contemplation*: Aristotle seems to have forgotten that most of the *NE* is concerned to show that moral virtue does indeed bring happiness (though not the higher form of happiness he thought came from contemplation).

89–96 Aristotle supports his view with reference to two wise men: Solon the early sixth-century Athenian statesman, and Anaxagoras, the fifth-century Presocratic philosopher.

89–91 *And Solon ... living sensibly*: taken from what Solon said to Croesus about Tellus (Herodotus 1.30).

98–102 *Therefore such a view has credibility ... reject what disagrees*: As often, Aristotle says that for proof in ethics we must look to the facts not to theories (cf. 1095b1 'One must begin from what is known').

103 *most loved by the gods*: because they regard such a person as being most like themselves.

10. Hippocratic *Sacred Disease* 1–6: Epilepsy

This extract is the first quarter of one of the most famous Greek medical writings, famous because in it the author, in explaining the causes of a disease traditionally identified with epilepsy, makes a devastating attack on magic and religion and in their place promotes a rational and intellectual approach to understanding the disease. The disease, the author says, is not caused by god, and those who try to cure it through purifications and rites designed to appease the god are charlatans; the disease has a natural cause, like any other disease, namely phlegm and bile entering the brain.

The view he rejects exemplifies a widespread Greek belief that an abnormal physical or mental condition, manifesting itself in abnormal behaviour or mental activity, is to be explained in terms of a force with a divine origin having entered the person, the condition being so abnormal for a human being that it must have a supernatural origin. So, for instance, poets with their great wisdom, skill and insight were inspired by the Muses; prophets, with their ability to see into the future, were inspired by a god, the Pythian priestess by the god of Pytho, Apollo; on the physical front, a victorious athlete at the Games had displayed such supernatural strength that he too was regarded as having received assistance from a god, as having temporarily transcended normal human status, in some cases as even being a god. In the case of epilepsy, the supernatural invasive force was regarded partly in mental and partly in physical terms. The author says that the charlatan purifiers to whom he is opposed use incantations (1.10, 2.13), but also purifications with a physical effect (avoidance of baths and certain foods, 2.13–14); the underlying idea is that the disease is a kind of god-sent dirt that can be washed or purged away. Particular manifestations of the disease were attributed to particular gods (4.21–33). Interestingly, although the author castigates these purifiers, the concept of purification forms an important part of his own explanation for the disease: it is, he says, caused when the body's natural purging processes, enabling phlegm to be expelled from the brain, malfunction (ch. 8). Moreover, the author, having ruled out the gods as causers of the disease, goes on to say (ch. 21) that the natural causes (heat, cold, winds) are themselves divine: 'The so-called sacred disease comes from the same causes as others, from things that enter and depart from the body, from cold, sun and from the changing restlessness of winds. These things are divine. So there is no need to put the disease in a special class and consider it more divine than others; they are all divine and human' (21.1–8). The thought here is in keeping with several Presocratic Ionian philosophers who sought natural causes for the nature of the world, but at the same time saw these natural causes as themselves divine. And although the purifiers' special dietetic recommendations are castigated, his rational explanations for their supposed efficacy show that he too was interested in how they worked. And he too at the end (21.24) recommends as a cure for epilepsy a diet that will effect changes in the amount of moist, dry, wet or cold in sufferers. But whereas the purifiers based many of their practices on taboos (see esp. 2.23–27: a sufferer must not wear black or a goat-skin, or put foot on foot or hand on hand), akin to some of the superstitious regulations prescribed by Hesiod (*Op.* 695–828) and Pythagorean cult, the author's suggestions as to causes, even if not correct, are at least in part derived from his own observations. He seems, for instance, to have made inferences from a post-mortem done on a goat (14.11–24): if you cut open the head of an epileptic goat, you will find the brain is moist and foul-smelling, 'whereby you may learn that it is not a god but the disease that injures the body' (cf. Plutarch *Pericles* 6.2 where Anaxagoras cuts open the head of a ram with only one horn and observes the unnatural position of the brain). As with the goat-condition, for humans too the Hippocratic author is describing a collection of *symptoms* which may not in every case be due to epilepsy as we would define it (viz. abnormal propagation of electrical activity in the brain); I owe this point and the Plutarch passage to Bob Sharples.

The author of the piece is unknown, but it probably belongs to the end of the 5th/beginning of the 4th century, and hence is one of many medical treatises attributed to Hippocrates of Cos (*c.* 460–370 B.C.) the greatest Greek doctor, though not necessarily by him. The text is uncertain in a number of places, but the general sense is always clear.

The whole passage is riddled with irony and sarcasm (cf. 2.35ff. on the Libyans) as the author denigrates the purifiers' charlatan practices.

Bibliography

G. E. R. Lloyd, *Magic, Reason and Experience* (Cambridge 1979) 15–28.

R. Parker, *Miasma* (Oxford 1983) 207–234 and index s.vv. 'Hippocrates', *Morb. Sacr.*

P. J. van der Eijk, 'The Theology of the Hippocratic Treatise *On the Sacred Disease*', *Apeiron* 23 (1990) 88–119, reprinted in id., *Medicine and Philosophy in Classical Antiquity* (Cambridge 2005) 45–73.

J. Longrigg, *Greek Medicine: From the Heroic to the Hellenistic Age* (London 1997).

1.

Concerning the so-called sacred disease the facts are as follows. It does not seem to me more divine than the other diseases or more sacred. But it has a nature and cause, though people thought it to be something divine out of inexperience and astonishment because it seems completely unlike
5   other phenomena. And because of their being at a loss to understand it, its divine nature continues to be accepted, but because of the ease of the method of cure by which they cure it, its divine nature is destroyed, because they cure it with purifications and incantations. If it is going to be thought divine because of the wonder it arouses, there will be many
10   sacred diseases and not just one, as I shall show that there are others that are no less amazing and extraordinary which no one thinks divine. On the one hand, fevers that occur every day or every other day or every third day seem to me to be no less sacred and no less arising through god than this disease, but they do not hold them in amazement; on the other
15   hand, I see people who are mad and mentally ill through no clear cause, and people who do many odd movements, and I know of many people who in their sleep groan and shout, and others who choke, and others who jump up and rush outside and are out of their mind until they wake up and are then healthy and sane just as they were before, though pale
20   and weak, and they act like this not once but often. There are many other symptoms of many sorts, but to speak about each of them would be a long story.

2.

The people who first called this disease sacred seem to me to be the sort who there are nowadays too, wizards and purifiers and begging priests and charlatans, people who pretend to be very pious and to know more than others. These people, excusing themselves by citing its sacredness
5   as a pretext for their inability to provide any beneficial treatment, and so that it should not be obvious that they knew nothing, regarded this affliction as sacred. And uttering suitable words they claimed a cure that would provide protection for themselves, applying purifications and incantations, and telling their patients to abstain from baths and many
10   foods unsuitable for sick people to eat, among sea-foods red-mullet, black-tail, mullet and eel (for these fish are the ones that most cause death), among meats goat, deer, pig and dog (for these meats are most liable to cause an upset stomach), among birds cock, dove and bustard,

and in addition all those regarded as very rich, among vegetables mint,
15   garlic and onions (for anything pungent is not beneficial to a sick
person); they also tell them not to wear a black cloak (for black is the
colour of death), nor to lie on or wear a goat-skin, nor to put foot on foot
or hand on hand (for they say that all these are inhibitory). They make
these regulations because of the divine, on the grounds that they know
20   better than other people, and claim other causes too, so that if the patient
becomes well, the reputation for cleverness should be theirs, but if he
dies their defence should be secure and they should have the excuse that
not they were responsible but the gods; for they did not give the patient
any medicine to eat or drink, nor did they dry him up with hot baths
25   so that they could seem to be responsible. I suppose that none of the
Libyans who live inland could be healthy because they lie on goatskins
and eat goat meat, since they do not have any blanket or cloak or shoe
which is not made from goat, for the only herds they have are goats and
oxen. But if these things when eaten and applied create and increase
30   the disease, and when not eaten cure it, then no longer is the god the
cause nor are the purifications beneficial, but it is the foods that are the
things curing and harming, and the power of the god disappears.

3.

For these reasons, therefore, those who undertake to cure these diseases
by this method seem to me to believe in neither sacred things nor gods.
For in cases where these diseases are removed through such purifications
and such treatment, what stops them arising and happening to people
5   through other means similar to these? So no longer the divine but
something human is the cause. For whoever is able to take away such
an affliction by purifying and bewitching, this person would also have
the means to inflict other conditions, and by this argument the divine
is destroyed. Saying and contriving such things they pretend to know
10   more than others, and they deceive people by prescribing for them
purifications and cleansings, and most of their talk comes down to god
and the divine. And yet in my view they do not seem to be talking about
piety, as they think, but about impiety rather, and how the gods do not
exist; and their piety and godliness is impious and unholy, as I shall
15   demonstrate.

4.

For if they claim to know how to bring down the moon, and to make the sun disappear, and to make storm and calm, and rains and droughts, and the sea uncrossable and the earth so it will not bear anything, and all other suchlike, whether those practising these skills say they can happen

5 by means of secret rites or some other scheme or practice they seem to me to be impious, and to believe the gods do not exist and have no power, and to be unlikely to refrain from any of the most extreme deeds in doing which how can they not be terrible in the eyes of the gods? For if a man by magic and sacrifice shall bring down the moon and make

10 the sun disappear and make storm and calm, I would not think any of these things divine, but man-made, if indeed the power of the god is overcome and enslaved by the intelligence of man. But perhaps this is not how it is, but rather men in need of a livelihood are contriving and fabricating many things of all sorts both with regard to this disease and

15 in all other respects, for each form of the disease laying the responsibility on a god. For if the afflicted imitate a goat, or if they roar, or if they have convulsions on the right side, they say the Mother of the Gods is the cause; if, rather, he makes a piercing and loud sound, they liken him to a horse and say Poseidon is responsible; if he defecates a bit,

20 as often happens under the pressure of the disease, the name Enodios is applied; if he does so more thinly and frequently like birds do, it is Apollo Nomios; if he emits foam from the mouth and kicks with his feet, Ares is the cause. Those whom in the course of the night fears and terrors assail and who have attacks of paranoia and jump from their beds and

25 rush outside, in such cases they say these are the assaults of Hecate and onslaughts of heroes. And they use purifications and incantations, and do somthing most unholy and ungodly, in my opinion. For they purify those in the grip of the disease with blood and other such things, as if they were in the grip of pollution, or guilty or bewitched by people or

30 had done some impious deed. They should have treated these people in the opposite way, sacrificing and praying and bringing them into sanctuaries and beseeching the gods. But as it is they do none of these things, but purify them. And some of the things they use for purifying they hide in the ground, some they throw into the sea, some they carry

35 away to the mountains where no one shall either touch or tread on them. They ought to have taken them to the sanctuaries and given them to the god, if god is the cause. I myself however do not think the body of a

man can be polluted by god, the most perishable by the most holy; but
even if it should happen to be polluted by something else or to suffer
40   something, it would be purified and cleansed by the god rather than
polluted. At least, it is god that purifies and cleanses the greatest and
most unholy of our sins and washes them from us, and we ourselves
point out the boundaries of the gods' sanctuaries and precincts so that
no one should cross them if they are not pure; and when we enter them
45   we sprinkle ourselves not as if we were polluting ourselves but with a
view to purifying ourselves in case we possess some earlier acquired
pollution. That is how it seems to me about purifications.

5.

But this disease seems to me no more divine than the rest, but has the
same essential nature as other diseases, and its cause is that from where
each other disease arises. And it is curable, and no less than the others,
unless it has become so strong after a long lapse of time that by now it is
5   stronger than the remedies being applied. Its origin, like that of other
diseases, is genetic. For if a phlegmatic child is born from a phlegmatic
parent, or a bilious one from a bilious parent, or a consumptive one from
a consumptive parent or a splenetic one from a splenetic parent, what
prevents any offspring being afflicted by whatever disease their mother
10   or father had? For the seed comes from everywhere in the body, healthy
seed from healthy parts and diseased seed from diseased parts. And
there is another strong proof that the disease is no more divine than
any other: for it afflicts those naturally phlegmatic, but does not attack
the bilious; and yet if it was more divine than the rest, this disease
15   should have come to all alike and not make a distinction between the
bilious and the phlegmatic.

6.

But the cause of this condition is the brain, as it is of the other most
serious diseases. In what way, and from what cause it comes, I shall
clearly set forth.

1.
2–3 *it has a nature and cause*: the Greek text is uncertain here, but the sense is clear.
8 *they cure it with purifications and incantations*: the author objects to the primitive
nature of the treatment provided by those who maintain the illness's divine origin.
Pindar (*Pythian* 3.51) says that Asclepius used charms as a means of healing.

12–14 *fevers ... amazement*: the author argues that fevers that occur every day, every other day, or every third day (perhaps malarial fevers whose regularity is due to the behaviour of the malarial parasite) should also be accounted divine because their occurring with such regularity is equally amazing and terrible.

15–16 *I see ... I know*: the author writes from personal experience.

2.

9 *telling their patients to abstain from baths*: abstention from baths as a form of purification is the opposite of the norm, but not unparalleled (Parker 215; for abstention from certain foods as a means of purifying oneself, see Parker 357–365). Bob Sharples points out that there is a question whether the author *himself* endorses the reasons given for abstaining from certain foods ('these fish are the ones that most cause death' *etc.*), for if he does, he is allowing some degree of legitimacy in his opponents' recommendations

10 *red-mullet*: commonly banned as its colour associated it with blood.

11 *black-tail*: the colour of death. The name 'black-tail' is simply a literal translation of the Greek name; it may be *Oblata melanurus* CV.

12–13 *For these meats are most liable to cause an upset stomach*: 'Dog, pig and goat: the three domestic animals that were commonly charged with scatophagy' (Parker 360).

13 *bustard*: a large running bird, like a goose. Pythagoreans, too, had restrictions concerning birds, *e.g.* 'Don't sacrifice a white cock' (D.L. 8.34).

16–18 *they also tell them not to ... or hand on hand*: taboos.

25–9 What is said of the Libyans implies a sarcastic 'modus tollens' argument: 'if A, then B; but not B, therefore not A'. Here, 'if goat-skins were a cause, none of the Libyans would be healthy; but they are healthy, so goat-skins are not a cause'. Lloyd (25) draws attention to the method of argument, and compares 5.11–16 below ('If the disease were divine it would attack all alike; but it does not do so, so it is not divine')

3.

So the author's conclusion is that in fact not even those who think the disease is god-caused have grounds for their claim that god is the cause, since (so the author hopes to have shown) even they adduce material causes (food, clothes *etc.*). He now continues this argument, saying that it is the human application of purifications *etc.* that can cause or remove diseases. Here the author's argument is that if a certain amount of purification can effect a cure, then it could also make matters worse; application and misapplication of *techne*, not the divine, is the cause.

12–14 *And yet in my view ... impious and unholy*: almost a *reductio ad absurdum* of his opponents' position.

4.

8 *in doing which how can they not be terrible in the eyes of the gods?*: text uncertain.
16–23 In some cases it is clear what the implicit connection is between god and symptom (Poseidon god of horses, Ares god of war), in others less so. Parker (244–5) suggests that the ability to cause wild disorder is what all these divinities (and heroes) have in common.
20 *Enodios*: epithet of Hecate.
21–2 *Apollo Nomios*: probably referring to Aristaeus, a demi-god of the countryside, son of Apollo (cf. Pindar, *Pythian* 9.64–5).
26 *heroes*: sometimes the ancient equivalent of trouble-makers or hooligans (Parker 243–5).
27–8 *For they purify ... with blood*: for purification by blood, see Parker 370–3: blood can easily be seen to be washed away; it can also stand as a token of the pollution to be removed (234).
33–4 *And some of the things they use for purifying ... throw into the sea*: Parker (210) compares *Il.* 1.314 where Chalcas tells the Achaeans to wash off their pollution and throw it into the sea; cf. also Theophrastus 16.29–30: the superstitious man purifies himself by the sea. The general idea is that salt-water purifies and the sea washes away (Parker 226–7).
41–7 Bob Sharples points out that the author is *accepting* conventional religious ideas here – at least rhetorically for the sake of his argument.

5.

1–3 *But this disease ... disease arises*: text uncertain, but in essence the author returns to and repeats what he said at the start (1.**1–5**).
4–5 *unless it has by now become so strong ... the remedies being applied*: the author recognises (correctly) that a chronic condition is generally less easily treated than a recent one.
5–6 *Its origin, like that of other diseases, is genetic*: a remarkable insight.
6–8 *phlegmatic, bilious, consumptive, splenetic*: to be interpreted literally, 'diseased with phlegm' *etc.*

11. *Lex Sacra* from Selinous: Pollution

This is a mid-5th-century B.C. inscription from Sicily detailing measures to be taken against pollution. It is inscribed in two columns, each written a different way up, on a lead tablet *c.* 60cm × 23cm. Its interest for this book lies in the rituals which people are instructed to perform to make contact with higher powers who can avert the perils of pollution. Column A reads more like a public proclamation, with instructions for sacrifices and libations on behalf of the state. Offerings are to be made to Zeus Eumenes, the Eumenides, and Zeus Meilichios

(A **9–10**) who had a cult at Selinous; and to the Tritopateres (A **11**), ancestral spirits who have been polluted and need to be cleansed. The instructions are sometimes addressed to people in the plural, sometimes made in the singular; this is probably an insignificant variation, just as in English one might say 'If anyone sees him, they're to call the police'. Column B is specifically about how to be purified from an *elasteros* (B **1, 12, 15**) = *alastōr*, 'spirit of vengeance'. The category of person addressed is perhaps a homicide (*autorrhektas* B **11**). A point of special interest in both columns is that part of the purification process seems to consist in a *theoxenia*, entertaining divinities with hospitality as if they were fellow-diners (A **17**, B **5**). Column B envisages the possibility of actually seeing one of these spirits. The point of these recommendations seems to be that the harmful spirits symbolise the polluted person's guilt, so when they are appeased both they and the guilty person are cleansed. In both A and B, after cleansing the spirits are more divine, the Tritopateres changing from heroes to gods (A **11–12, 21**), the *elasteroi* becoming immortals (B **15**). This process has similarities with the deification of Empedocles (see Fr. 112), also from Sicily, a part of the Greek world strongly associated with Pythagorean theories of metempsychosis. However, as North in his review article makes clear, considerable uncertainty over interpretation and the context of the regulations must remain.

Selinous came under Carthaginian control in 409 B.C.; prior to that it was an independent Greek city state. The present text shows no Punic influence and in ethos is in keeping with traditional Greek religious thought. The instructions are most similar to those detailed in a similar *lex sacra*, from Cyrene (See R. Parker, *Miasma* 332–351). It is unclear what prompted the publication of these regulations (bloodshed seems the most likely candidate, but it could have been disease; death of any kind was potentially a source of pollution).

Although the instructions are detailed, they give considerable freedom to the agents (A **26**: 'Let him invite who he wishes', and esp. B **2–3, 8**). This freedom, Col. A's concern with Tritopateres (and *homosepuoi*, 'those of the same family', **3**), suggesting that the instructions are geared to the *oikos*, not the state as a whole, and the *theoxeniae*, all combine to suggest that whatever level of authority issued the regulations, a personal approach to solving religious problems was deemed most effective.

Both this introduction and the notes that follow are heavily indebted to the comprehensive edition of the text by Jameson, Jordan and Kotansky, and the review article on that edition by J. North (both mentioned below). The translation below is taken from their edition (with some changes).

Bibliography

A *Lex Sacra* from Selinous, Michael H. Jameson, David R. Jordan, Roy D. Kotansky, Greek, Roman, and Byzantine Monographs 11 (Duke University, Durham, North Carolina 1993).

J. North, *Scripta Classica Israelica* 15 (1996) 293–301 (review article 'Pollution and Purification at Selinous').

Column A

3   ... them leaving behind ... those of the same family must burn in the sacrificial by fire.

7   ...... of the holy things. The sacrifices (are to be performed) before (the festival of) the Kotytia and before the truce every fifth year whenever the Olympic festival occurs. To Zeus Eumenes and the Eumenides

10   sacrifice a full-grown sheep, and to Zeus Meilichios in the precinct of Myskos a full-grown sheep. Sacrifice to the Tritopateres, the impure ones, as to the heroes, having poured a libation of wine through the roof, and burn one of the ninth parts. Let those to whom it is permitted perform a sacrifice, consecrate with fire, sprinkle with water the people

15   gathered round and anoint with oil. And then let them sacrifice a full-grown sheep to the now pure Tritopateres. Pouring down a libation of honey-mixture, let him set out both a table and a couch; and let him put on them a pure cloth, and crowns of olive, (15) and honey-mixture in new cups, and cakes and meat. And having made the offerings, let them

20   burn them, and let them anoint the cups and put them on the table. Let them perform the ancestral sacrifices as to the gods. To Zeus Meilichios in the precinct of Euthydamos let them sacrifice a ram. And may it be possible to sacrifice again after a year. Let him take out the sacred objects – the public ones – and place a table in front of them, and burn a

25   thigh and the first-fruits from the table and (20) the bones. Let no meat be carried out of the precinct. Let him invite whoever he wishes. And let it also be possible to sacrifice after a year at home. Let them slaughter ... of the statues. Let them sacrifice whatever sacrifice the ancestral customs permit ... in the third year.

Column B

If a man wishes to be purified from *elasteroi*, having made a proclamation from wherever he wishes and whenever in the year he wishes and in whatever month he wishes and on whatever day he wishes, having made

the proclamation to whatever locality he wishes, let him purify himself.
5   On receiving him, let him give him water for him to wash with, and a
meal and salt to the same. And having sacrificed a piglet (5) to Zeus, let
him go from the sanctuary and turn round. And let him be addressed and
take food for himself and sleep wherever he wishes. If anyone wishes to
purify himself with respect to a foreign or family one, whether one he
10   has merely heard of or one he has actually seen or anyone else at all, let
him purify himself in the same way as the *autorrhektas* does when he
is purified of an *elasteros*. Having (10) sacrificed a full-grown sheep on
the public altar, let him be pure. Having marked a boundary with salt and
sprinkled with water using a golden vessel, let him go away. Whenever
15   one needs to sacrifice to the *elasteros*, sacrifice as to the immortals. But
let him slaughter the victim so its blood flows into the earth.

Column A

3 The first three lines of the inscription are damaged, and lines 4–6 have been
erased.

7–9 *The sacrifices ... occurs*: The time indicated is early summer. The Olympic
Games were held every four years according to the way we count, but every five
years according to the inclusive way the Greeks counted (*e.g.* 2008, 2009, 2010,
2011, 2012). The Kotyt(t)ia was a Sicilian festival, in honour of the obscure goddess
Kotyto, in which nuts and cakes were fastened to branches for people to grab.
Because of the poor state of the text in the early part of the inscription, it is not clear
exactly what sacrifices are being referred to here.

9–11 *To Zeus Eumenes ... precinct of Myskos*: the Kindly Zeus, the Kindly Ones
and the Mild Zeus, all divinities of the Underworld invoked to placate the spirits of
the dead, especially following bloodshed. A late-seventh-century gravestone of a
Myskos is known from Selinous; the Myskos in our text may be a descendant.

11 *Tritopatres*: ancestors, perhaps ones going back three generations. Here they seem
to be in particular ancestral spirits, apparently polluted by some form of subsequent
family death, who must be purified and placated by wine offerings (Jameson, Jordan
and Kotansky 107–114): if x kills y, then not only x but also x's ancestral spirits are
polluted, but like x they too can be purified and change from impure to pure.

12–13 *through the roof*: sc. of a structure built in honour of the Tritopateres, so the
liquid would filter down to them.

burn one of the ninth parts: a ninth part of each of the two sacrifices just mentioned
(7–11) could be burnt for the Tritopateres. Offerings of ninth parts are common,
sometimes denoted by the special Greek verb *enateuein*, lit. 'to ninth'.

15 *anoint with oil*: sc. stones symbolising the Tritopateres, or the altar.

15–16 *And then ... now pure Tritopateres*: Now that the Tritopateres have been
purified, and thus placated, they get another sacrifice.

16–21 *Pouring down a libation ... as to the gods*: These lines describe a Theoxenia, when the gods were thought to come to one's house and were welcomed with a meal; cf. Burkert, *Greek Religion* 107, Jameson, Jordan and Kotansky 67–70.

20 *and let them anoint the cups and put them on the table*: it is unclear exactly what procedure is envisaged; probably, the anointing was done to purify the cups.

22 *Euthydamos*: this Euthydamos is otherwise unknown, but evidently comparable to Myskos (above 10).

23 *again ... after a year*: if he feels the need for another placatory sacrifice.

23–4 *the sacred objects – the public ones*: there seems to be a distinction between these sacred objects and the previously mentioned ancestral (private) ones.

25 *thigh*: an especially revered portion.

25–6 *Let no meat be carried out of the precinct*: the meat is to be eaten by everyone together at the place of sacrifice, increasing the bond with the gods.

Column B

This column is concerned with private purificatory rites which can be made at any time

1 *elasteroi*: avengers, usually in the form of hostile, supernatural spirits of dead people that take revenge on murderers.

5–6 *On receiving him let him ... to the same*: The idea seems to be that the guilty person placates the avenging spirit when it visits him by offering it water, food and salt to cleanse away the spirit's wrath. One might have expected the guilty person to have been cleansed by means of the water and salt (cf. Jameson, Jordan and Kotansky 56 n.2), but the procedure is paralleled in the *Lex Sacra* from Cyrene (J., J. and K. 54–5, 76)

6–7 *And having sacrificed a piglet ... turn round*: He sacrifices a piglet to Zeus (Meilichios) and can then withdraw cleansed from Zeus' shrine and get on with his life as normal. 'Let him go ... and turn round' seems to mean 'let him turn round and go'.

8–12 *If anyone ... elasteros*: For various possible interpretations of this sentence, see North's review article 295–7. The precise meaning of the word *autorrhektas* is uncertain but is probably 'homicide'; if so, then what has preceded in this column of the inscription and in Column A would seem to relate to purifications necessary for people guilty of bloodshed in general though not specifically homicides (although, as North suggests 228–9, *e.g.* disease or infertility believed to have been brought about by hostile spirits are other possibilities for the general context).

12–13 *Having sacrificed ... let him be pure*: It is now made explicit that the guilty one, though an individual persecuted by (probably) an individual's avenging spirit, requires purification with a public dimension.

13–14 *Having marked a boundary ... let him go away*: Apparently he separates himself from the altar at which he has sacrificed, and which has now relieved him of his guilt, sprinkling salt (a purifying agent) between himself and the altar.

14–16 *Whenever ... earth*: 'So the *elasteroi* are divine, but chthonic, powers by the end of B. The shift is from spirits that appear to be close to human beings, acting on their behalf or pursuing their murderers, to beings who receive sacrifice, and are to be treated, if not quite as gods, at any rate as divine figures of some kind. It makes it clear above all how ritual performed by human beings can change the status, as well as the benevolence, of suprahuman beings and raises fundamental questions about the Greek conception of deity in general' (North 299–300).

12, 13 and 14: ORPHISM

Orphism was one type of Bacchic or Dionysiac cult, that focussed on the afterlife and promised to initiates a new life, even divinity, after requisite purification. Many details are unclear just because it was mystery cult shrouded in secrecy. In its focus on the afterlife it has much in common with Pythagoreanism, and in many respects it is difficult to distinguish the two sects. Its central tenet was that initiation into the cult could annul sins of the past and enable the deceased to be purified, escape punishment and be reborn into a higher form of existence. To validate this tenet Orphics created a number of rebirth myths, especially one in which Dionysus was dismembered by the Titans but reborn, and from the soot of the Titans when they had been blasted by Zeus' thunderbolt mortals, inheriting the Titans' guilt, were born. Such Dionysiac myths were a paradigm for their own beliefs. (For a different view, attacking the myth of Dionysus and the Titans as a late antique fabrication, see R. G. Edmonds, 'Tearing apart the Zagreus myth: a few disparaging remarks on Orpheus and original sin', *Classical Antiquity* 18 (1999), 35–73).

Orphism was not a fringe or marginal sect: the scattered locations where the gold leaves have been found show how widespread it was. But in contrast to mainstream Greek civic religion, with mass-participation festivals on set days, it appealed to the individual and promised individual salvation. It seems to have had both a private and a public dimension, with personal initiation followed by a public manifestation of the worshippers (cf. Hdt. 4.79, Hipponion Gold Leaf **15–16**). It is just because the personal, individual, side of it was so central to the initiation that secrecy was so important and we know relatively little about details of the cult. For an excellent survey of Orphism, see R. Parker, 'Early Orphism', in *The Greek World* ed. A. Powell (London 1995), 483–510.

12. Orphism (1): Herodotus 4.78.3–4.80.5, Scyles and Olbia

This story about Scyles king of Scythia in the mid-5th century B.C. illustrates both the opposition between Greeks and barbarians, but also and more importantly for this book, the place Orphism within a Bacchic cult, that is worship of Dionysus, could have for an individual. The connection between Orphism and Bacchism was for a long time denied by scholars, but the bone tablets discovered at Olbia (see below) and the tablet from Hipponion (see **Text 13.1**, line **16**) confirm it.

The story is one of two told by Herodotus to show how strongly the barbarian Scythians objected to anyone, even their king, adopting Greek practices. In the first story, the sixth-century Scythian Anacharsis is said to have been put to death for worshipping the Greeks Mother goddess Cybele (Hdt. 4.76). In this second story Scyles is put to death for his participation in the Greek cult of Bacchus. The main part of the story is set by the Scythian river Borysthenes at the city of Olbia (not named in our passage, but see 4.18.1: '... Scythian farmers who the Greeks living on the River Hypanis call Borysthenites, while they call themselves people of Olbia.'). The importance of the Bacchic cult there is confirmed by bone tablets which may have served as ID cards for members of the cult. Writing on them gives an insight into what the cult offered. One has written on it 'Life, death, life; truth; Dio(nysus); Orphics,' another 'Peace, War; truth, falsity; Dio(nysus)', a third 'Dio(nysus); truth; soul'. There is an account of these tablets and their implications by M. L. West in the article in *ZPE* mentioned above: 'They [the graffiti] tell us that the initiates rejoiced in specially revealed knowledge, ἀλήθεια [truth], connected with the soul and with a life after death, and that they honoured the name of the prophet Orpheus' (26). From the fifth century such cults were quite common, mostly located on the periphery of the Greek world, as evidenced by the Orphic gold leaves, more elaborate than the bone plates of Olbia but serving a similar function, found at a number of sites mainly in northern Greece, southern Italy, Sicily and Crete. The cults provided an alternative to organised state religious festivals, offering through personal initiation to purify their members of their earthly sins, give them a special knowledge of the truth about the immortality of the soul, and thereby enable them to escape the terrors of the underworld and be reborn. Herodotus' description of Scyles shows that the cult at Olbia was open to foreigners and included a public side consisting in revelling through the city in an orgy manifesting the feeling of release provided by the doctrinal side. It was not held in secret and it was not a fringe phenomenon, nor did it preclude other religious worship (Scyles honoured the gods according to Greek custom, 13). It is ironic that it was initiation into a cult promising an afterlife that led to his death. That there was something not quite right about Scyles' participation in the cult (a Scythian foreigner publicly flaunting it) is hinted at by Herodotus in his usual dispassionate manner when he says (23–5) that on the night before his initiation his house was struck by lightning, but nevertheless he carried on with it.

Bibliography

M. L. West, 'The Orphics of Olbia', *Zeitschrift für Papyrologie und Epigraphik* 45 (1982) 17–29.

W. Burkert, *Ancient Mystery Cults* (Harvard 1987).

4.78

When he was ruling the Scythians Scyles in no way liked the Scythian way of life, but he was much more attracted towards Greek things from the education he had received, and he used to do the following. Whenever he led the army of the Scythians to the city of the Borysthenites (and
5   these Borysthenites say that they are Milesians), whenever Scyles came to these people, he used to leave his army on the outskirts, and he himself when he came to the city-wall, entered and locked the gates behind him, having taken off his Scythian clothes he would put on Greek clothing, and wearing this he walked around with neither any spear-
10 bearers in attendance nor anyone else (they guarded the gates, lest any of the Scythians should see that he was wearing this clothing), and he did everything else in a Greek way and even made offerings to the gods according to Greek custom. Whenever he had passed a month or more than this he would depart and put on his Scythian clothing. He used to
15 do this many times, and built himself a house by the Borysthenes and married a local woman to live in it.

4.79

But when the time came for him to meet with misfortune, it came about for the following reason. He had a desire to be initiated into the Bacchic rites of Dionysus, and just as he was about to undertake the
20 initiation, a very great portent occurred. In the city of the Borysthenites he owned an area consisting in a large and very expensive home, which I mentioned a little before, round which stood sphinxes and griffins

made of marble. Against this house the god hurled a bolt of lightning. And although the whole house was burnt down, Scyles nonetheless went through with the initiation. Scythians reproach the Greeks over Bacchic worship, for they say it is not right to invent a god like this who leads people to be mad. When Scyles had been initiated into the Bacchic rites, one of the Borysthenites ran off towards the Scythians saying, 'You laugh at us, O Scythians, because we practise Bacchic rites and the god possesses us: now this god has taken hold of your own king, and he is behaving like a bacchant and is maddened by the god. If you do not believe me, follow me and I shall show you'. The leading men of the Scythians followed, and the Borysthenite led them secretly up to a tower and sat them down. When Scyles passed by with his band of Bacchic followers and the Scythians saw him being a bacchant, they very much considered it a great mishap, and having gone out from the city they revealed to the whole army all that they had seen.

4.80

Afterwards, when Scyles was marching out his army into his own land, the Scythians sought the protection of his brother Octamasades, the son of Teres' daughter, and revolted from Scyles. He, having learnt what was happening to himself and the reason it was being done, fled to Thrace. When Octamasades found this out, he marched to Thrace. When he was by the Ister, the Thracians opposed him. When they were about to join battle, Sitalces sent a messenger to Octamasades to say the following: 'Why do we need to fight each other? You are the son of my sister, and you have my brother. You give him back to me, and I'll hand over your brother Scyles to you. You don't risk your army, and I won't either.' By means of the messenger Sitalces made these proposals of peace (for Sitalces' brother was with Octamasades, having fled from Sitalces). Octamasades agreed to these proposals, and having handed over to Sitalces his brother, Octamasades' uncle on his mother's side, took his own brother Scyles. Sitalces took his brother and led him away. But Octamasades beheaded Scyles right there. So closely do the Scythians guard their own customs, while to those who acquire in addition foreign practices such punishments do they give.

2–3 *from the education he had received*: Herodotus says earlier (78.1) this was from his mother who was not a Scythian, but came from Istria, south of Olbia on the Black Sea, and taught him Greek.

4 *city of the Borysthenites*: Olbia, at the mouth of the River Borysthenes on the Black Sea, one of many colonies on the Black Sea founded by Miletus.

8 *Scythian clothes*: typically including trousers and hat.

12–13 *made offerings to the gods according to Greek custom*: for Scythian religious practice, see 4.59–62: Dionysus, or the Scythian equivalent, was not among the deities worshipped in Scythia, according to Herodotus.

18–19 *the Bacchic rites of Dionysus*: cf. **34–5** below, where Scyles is part of an orgiastic *thiasos* (band of revellers), ecstatic and possessed by the god. The basic message of Bacchic cults was *lysis* or release from care.

21–3 *a large and very expensive home ... sphinxes and griffins made of marble*: emphasising Scyles' extravagance and how to some extent his doom was deserved.

25 *initiation*: a mystical ceremony; see Burkert 96–7.

26–7 *leads people to be mad*: *enthousiasmos* (possession by the god) was a key element in Dionysiac religion, vividly dramatised in Euripides' *Bacchae*.

38 *Afterwards* ... This chapter may be a later addition, as Sitalces, king of the Odrysians of Thrace, is mentioned without introduction.

39–40 *the son of Teres' daughter*: Teres was the father of Sitalces.

13. Orphism (2): Gold Leaves, a Selection

More than 30 gold leaves, dating from the late fifth century BC to the 2nd century AD, have been discovered, mainly in northern Greece, south Italy, Sicily and Crete. Most are rectangular, a few centimetres in size, though some are shaped like leaves; the writing is very small (photographs in the edition by Pugliese Carratelli). They were found in graves, folded and buried along with the deceased. There is a family resemblance between them, with wording shared between them. In some places words and line order seem to have resulted from the scribe, probably an illiterate slave who was not a cult member and did not understand what he was writing, mis-remembering what he was meant to be inscribing and remembering sounds rather than sense, thereby conflating and abbreviating lines. The leaves are rightly called Orphic and regarded as evidence for Orphism because some of their main themes, life after death, Dionysus and Bacchus recur together with the word 'Orphic' on the similar bone plates from Olbia (see above). Most of the leaves seem to have functioned as tokens or passwords, reminding the dead person what he should do and say in the Underworld to ensure his re-birth. Although the obscurity of what they say has been compounded by the scribal errors, Orphics belonged to a mystic sect and riddling obscurity served to keep the truth secret from non-members. No plates have been found in Attica, because there the Eleusinian Mysteries were the dominant mystery cult.

Bibliography

R. G. Edmonds, 'Tearing apart the Zagreus myth: a few disparaging remarks on Orpheus and original sin', *Classical Antiquity* 18 (1999), 35–73.

G. Pugliese Carratelli, *Le Lamine d'Oro Orfiche* (Milan 2001) (French translation by A.-Ph. Segonds and C. Luna: Les Lamelles d'Or Orphiques (Paris, 2003).

J. N. Bremmer, *The Rise and Fall of the Afterlife* (London 2002).

R. G. Edmonds, *Myths of the Underworld Journey: Plato, Aristophanes, and the 'Orphic' Gold Tablets* (Cambridge, 2004).

F. Graf and S. I. Johnston, *Ritual Texts for the Afterlife. Orpheus and the Bacchic Gold Tablets* (Abingdon 2007).

A. Bernabé and A. I. Jiménez San Christóbal, *Instructions for the Netherworld. The Orphic Gold Tablets* (tr. M. Chase) (Leiden and Boston 2008).

1. Tablet from Hipponion (= Vibo Valentia), Calabria, South Italy (*c.* 400 BC) (Pug. Car. I A 1, G.-J. 1)
There is a detailed commentary on this tablet in Bernabé and Jiménez San Christóbal 9–59.

> This is the task(?) of Memory, when he is about to die,
> Into the well-fitted house of Hades. There is on the right a spring,
> And standing by it a shining cypress.
> Going down here souls of the dead are cooled.
> 5   Do not even go near this spring.
> Further on you will find cold water flowing forth
> From the pool of Memory; guards stand over it.
> They will ask you with their wise minds
> Why you search out the darkness of gloomy Hades.
> 10   Say, 'I am a child of Earth and starry Heaven.
> I am parched and dying from thirst. But give me quickly
> Cold water to drink from the pool of Memory.'
> And they will speak to the queen of the Underworld,
> And they will give you water to drink from the pool of Memory.
> 15   And having drunk you go along the holy road which other
> Glorious initiates and worshippers of Bacchus travel also.

1 The word translated 'task' is a conjecture. If correct, the sense is 'When you are about to die and go into Hades, what you need to remember (to be re-born) is as follows'. This tablet, like many of the others, seems to have functioned as a mnemonic device for the initiate in order for the purity and divinity of his soul (as that of an initiate) to be recognised and for him thereby to qualify for a glorious rebirth. Exactly how it functioned is unclear; Bob Sharples suggests the idea might be 'either (a) that he should memorise the instructions when about to die, but the tablet is a back-up in case his post-mortem memory fails, or else (b) that in some way written tablets are for the dead as conscious remembering is for the living'.

2 *Into*: again the Greek is uncertain.

3 *cypress*: a tree with funerary overtones – coffins were made from its wood (Thuc. 2.34.3).

4 *souls of the dead are cooled*: i.e. refreshed and reinvigorated for a return to the upper world. But this spring is not for initiates and will not bring bliss. The geography of the Underworld, with its two sources of water, serves to distinguish the uninitiated (who are impure and destined for a rebirth into a painful, lowly form of existence) and the pure initiates who alone will be reborn into a blissful, higher form of existence.

7 *pool of Memory*: the idea seems to be that by drinking from the pool of Memory the initiate demonstrates that he is mindful of his purity and of what he has learnt as an initiate. Memory was important to Pythagoras: he is said to have been able to remember everything, including having been Euphorbus during the Trojan War thus proving he had a previous existence (see *Early Greek Philosophy* ed. J. Barnes (Harmondsworth, 1987), 86–7; Empedocles, too, remembered having once been a boy, a girl, a bush, a bird and a fish (**Text 7, Fr. 117** = *EGP* 196).

8 *with their wise minds*: a Homeric formula.

10 *I am a child of Earth and starry heaven*: I have an earthly and a divine nature, like the Orphics' revered god Dionysus, son of Zeus and Semele, concerning whom the Orphics to justify their own beliefs created a mythology according to which Dionysus was torn apart by the Titans and reborn; Zeus blasted the Titans with his thunderbolt and from their ashes humans were born – hence the innate wickedness of humans which Orphics believed their religion could nullify.

13 *queen of the Underworld*: Persephone (cf. next tablet, line **7**).

15–16 *the holy road which other/Glorious initiates and worshippers of Bacchus travel also*: you will have a higher, divine existence. The wording perhaps alludes to a procession that was part of Orphic ritual, and presents Orphism as a type of Bacchic cult (one that in particular used writing and books, as opposed to the frenzied madness of the type of Bacchic cult dramatised in Euripides *Bacchae*).

2. Tablet from Thurii, Lucania, South Italy (4th century BC)
(Pug. Car. II B 1, G.-J. 3)
There is a detailed commentary on this tablet in Bernabé and Jiménez San
Christóbal 99–132.

> I come pure from the pure, Queen of the Underworld,
> Eucles, Eubouleus, and you other immortal gods.
> For I too claim to belong to your blessed family.
> But Fate overcame me and the thundering Lightning-thrower.
>   other immortal gods.
> 5   But I flew out of the grievous round of heavy pain,
> And with swift feet stepped onto the crown I longed for,
> And sank beneath the breast of the Underworld Queen,
> And with swift feet stepped onto the crown I longed for.
> 'Happy and blessed, you will be a god instead of a mortal.'
> 10 A kid I fell into milk.

1 *I come*: If the text printed here is correct, then the dead initiate's soul is speaking in the Underworld in its quest to gain a blissful, divine next existence.

2 *Eucles, Eubouleus*: Hades, Dionysus. 'other immortal gods' is an epic formula.

3 *I too claim to belong to your blessed family*: cf. line **10** in the first tablet above, 'I am a child of Earth and starry Heaven'.

4–5 I died, and having entered a painful cycle of death and re-birth, escaped it (by becoming a pure initiate and seeing the truth) and have now reached my longed-for goal of bliss thanks to the Queen of the Underworld recognising my purity and divinity. The tablet gives two alternative endings to line **4**; the latter has been remembered from line **2**. The first part of line **4** is a Homeric formula (*e.g. Il.* 18.119). For the painful cycle of birth and re-birth experienced by the impure, cf. Empedocles Fr. 115.8.

6 Note the athletics metaphor: both the initiate and the athletics victor achieve bliss and an elevated status.

8 An unnecessary remembering of line **6**.

9 Making explicit that the initiate can acquire divine bliss and be a god. Cf. Empedocles **Text 7, Fr. 112.4**: I am an immortal god, no longer mortal.

10 *A kid I fell into milk*: probably a metaphorical way of describing the final bliss of the initiate: it is like milk to a baby goat. Other tablets (from Pelinna in Thessaly) mention as variations on the idea a bull jumping into milk and a ram falling into milk.

14. Orphism (3): The Derveni Papyrus (selected fragments)

The Derveni Papyrus takes its name from Derveni, near Thessaloniki, where it was found in 1962, partially burnt in a tomb. It was probably written in the second half of the fourth century BC, and is therefore one of the earliest surviving examples of Greek writing on papyrus. It contains a commentary on Orphic ritual practices and on a poem attributed to Orpheus. The author of the commentary is unknown, but was well acquainted with Presocratic philosophy, and in his commentary through allegory he re-interprets the Orphic text into Presocratic terms. The Orphic poem itself, as far as one can tell from the excerpts quoted by the commentator, has much in common with other Orphic rhapsodies, and tells of the origin of the world and birth of the gods. Described as 'the most important new piece of evidence about Greek philosophy and religion to come to light since the Renaissance' (R. Janko, *Bryn Mawr Classical Review* 2005.01.27, reviewing Betegh), the papyrus belongs to a tradition of allegorical interpretation of poetry going back to Theagenes of Rhegium in the late 6th century BC, continuing into the fifth century and perhaps including some sophists. The author introduces Orpheus as a riddling allegorist in Column 7 and in Col. 14, for example, equates Cronus with Mind (the controlling power in Anaxagoras' philosophical system, to which the author is heavily indebted) and explains the etymology of 'Cronus' as from the Greek *krouesthai* 'to thrust', because Cronus/Mind 'thrust' the elements against each other. 'He has a preconceived system to which he is determined to fit Orpheus and everything else. The consequence is that his interpretations are uniformly false. Not once does he come near to giving a correct explanation of anything in his text' (West, 79).

It is hard to be certain of the author's purpose. The fact that he had access to an Orphic text and was prepared to write about it suggests he was a member of an Orphic sect himself whose function was to explain and elucidate traditional Orphic poetry to initiates; this he does by 'translating' it into the terms of Presocratic philosophy with which he was familiar.

Twenty-six incomplete columns of writing survive on the papyrus; how many are missing is not known.

(Texts and translations after Janko *ZPE* 141 (2002) 1–62),

Bibliography
M. L. West, *The Orphic Poems* (Oxford 1983) 68–113,
A. Laks and G. W. Most, *Studies on the Derveni Papyrus* (Oxford 1997),

E. Hussey, 'The Enigmas of Derveni', in *Oxford Studies of Ancient Philosophy* 17 (1999) 303–24,

G. Betegh, *The Derveni Papyrus: Cosmology, Theology and Interpretation* (Cambridge 2004),

Col. 6

The author is here attempting to interpret ritual offerings to spirits of the dead, explaining that the reason why Orphics sacrifice and make offerings to daimons and the Eumenides is to offer recompense and placate avenging souls of the dead. The eschatological context links it to Orphism. In the previous Column the author castigates people for not understanding dream-visions that might help them overcome the terrors of Hades, and in Column 20 (below) he has a go at the general ignorance of initiates who do not understand the rites in which they participate. In general, he thinks people are misguided and need his enlightenment. In this respect he is like Heraclitus: 'Most people do not understand the things they encounter, nor do they know what they have learned, but they think they do' (B17). He quotes Heraclitus in Col. 4, and doubtless approved of his style of writing, riddling and in need of interpretation like (in his view) that of the Orphic poem he interprets.

> ... prayers and sacrifices placate the souls. An incantation by *magoi* can dislodge daimons that become a hindrance; daimons that are a hindrance are avenging souls. The *magoi* perform the sacrifice for this reason, as if they are paying a penalty. Onto (5) the offerings they make libations
> 5   of water and milk, with both of which they also make drink-offerings. They sacrifice cakes which are countless and many-humped, because the souls too are countless. Initiates make a first sacrifice to the Eumenides in the same way as the *magoi* do; for the Eumenides are souls. Hence, a person who intends to sacrifice to the gods first ... of a bird ...

1 *magoi*: religious experts, Orphic priests.
2 *daimons*: spirits of the dead, equated by the author with avenging souls of the dead and (7) the Eumenides.
3 *avenging souls*: the Erinyes of Col. 2. The author explains that Erinyes are really avenging souls. Below (7) he explains the Eumenides as souls. In his allegorical interpretations he does away with the mythological figures.
6–7 *cakes which are countless ... souls too are countless*: the author explains why so many cakes are offered.
9 bird: bird sacrifice is unexpected. The author may have gone on to explain that they sacrifice a bird because souls are winged (Janko).

Col. 7

This Column marks the start of the author's commentary on the Orphic poem.

> ... hymn saying sound and permissible things. For [he was speaking allegorically] with his poetry, and he was not able to state what the words referred to and their meaning. His poetry is something alien and riddling for people (5). But Orpheus did not want to tell them unbelievable
> 5 things in riddles, but important things in riddles. In fact he is speaking allegorically from his very first word right through to his last, as he makes clear also in the well-known verse. For when he orders them to 'close their doors' (10) on their ears, he means he is not making rules for the many but instructing those [pure in hearing]

1ff 'He (Orpheus) actually composed a meaningful hymn (= 'poem') for those permitted to hear it, provided you understand it as allegory in the way I explain it.'
8 *close their doors*: the first line of the poem on which the author is commenting almost certainly ended 'close your doors, ye profane', and began with something like 'I sing to those permitted to listen'. This is a traditional formula to indicate that only the initiated may see or listen.

In Cols. 13 and 14 the author continues his cosmological interpretation of the Orphic poem. Interpretation of the first four lines of Column 13 is controversial (a detailed discussion in Betegh 111–122) but may refer to a primordial act of swallowing by Zeus of the penis of Uranus (a conflation of the version in Hesiod's *Works and Days* where Cronus severs Uranus' genitals and swallows his children), following a prophecy by Night. The author claims that what was separated was in fact the sun. Col. 14 continues discussing the sun and introduces the role of Mind

Col. 13

> (5) Since (Orpheus) is giving hints about reality throughout his poetry, one must discuss it verse by verse. He used this verse, likening the sun to a genital organ, because he saw that people think that generation resides in genitals, and does not arise without genitals. For without the sun it
> 5 would have been impossible for the things that exist to have come to be as they are, and when the things that exist had come about ... the sun (10) ...everything ... (the verse) 'to him by Earth Cronus was born, who did a great deed' ... (so that it can)

1–2 Explicit justification by the author for his allegorical method of interpretation.

Col 14

made the brightest and hottest element 'leap forth', once it had been
separated from itself. So (Orpheus) is saying that this 'Cronus' 'by
Earth was born' to the sun, because he caused the elements to be 'thrust'
(*krouesthai*) against each other on account of the sun. This is why
5   (Orpheus) says 'he who did a great deed'. The next verse: 'Uranus
son of Night, he who first was king'. After (Orpheus) has named Mind
(*Nous*) 'Cronus' because he 'thrust' (*krouonta*) the elements against one
another, he states that he 'did a great deed to Uranus: for he states that
(Uranus) had his kingship taken away. (Orpheus) named him 'Cronus'
10   after his action, and the other elements in accordance with the same
principle. For ... of all the things that exist ..., as (Orpheus) sees their
nature ... he is stating that (Uranus) had his kingship taken away when
the things that exist were (thrust together) ...

1–2 *the brightest ... itself*: Cronus' castration of Uranus is interpreted as the separation
of the sun from the other cosmic bodies.
2–5 *So ...deed*: essentially an allegorical interpretation of Cronus, deriving his
name and role from *krouō* 'thrust': after the sun was created, the other elements
thrust against one another, and this 'thrusting' gave rise to Cronus. It is illogical that
Cronus is both the cause of the sun (through his castration of Uranus), and born to
the sun; the solution, if need be, must be that the Cronus of the myth is different
from the Cronus as understood by the author (n.b. *this* 'Cronus') (Betegh 123)
6–7 The author is explicit that Cronus is really Mind. In Col. 16 he goes even further:
'he [Orpheus] makes clear that the Mind itself, being alone, is worth everything, as
if the other things were nothing. For it would not be possible for the things that
exist to be such without the Mind'. This primacy of Mind is ultimately derived
from the fifth-century Presocratic philosopher Anaxagoras for whom Mind is pure,
infinite and starts off the process of cosmogony: 'Mind is something infinite and
self-controlling, and it has been mixed with no thing but is alone by itself ...For
it is the finest of all things and the purest, and it possesses all knowledge about
everything, and it has the greatest strength' (B 12). The rest of Col. 14 elaborates
on the 'great deed' done by Cronus, the castration of Uranus, which sparked off the
thrusting process that created the universe, the magnitude of this deed justifying
Cronus' equation by the author with Mind.

Col 20

Here the author resumes his tirade against people who do not understand the true meaning of the rituals in which they participate . He contrasts two classes of people: those who have been initiated after merely seeing the rites, and those who have been initiated after paying a professional consultant; the former are merely foolish, the latter foolish and pitiable (because they have wasted their money). The implication is that what both classes of initate really need is the author's true understanding of their rites.

The whole passage may be compared with Plato *Republic* 364–5, where Plato scathingly refers to itinerant prophets who for a fee claim to be able to provide spells, incantations and books of ritual instruction for ridding people of their sins and preparing them for the next world.

> I am less amazed that those people who have merely seen the rites and been initiated in the cities do not comprehend them; for it is impossible simultaneously to hear what is said and to understand it. But those who (have been initiated) by someone who is a professional in the rites are
> 5 worthy of amazement and (5) pity: amazement because, although they suppose, before they perform the rites, they will have knowledge, they go away after having performed them before obtaining knowledge, and make no further enquiries, as if they actually knew something about what they saw, heard or learned; and pity because it is not enough for them
> 10 that they have paid beforehand a fee, (10) but they go away deprived of their good sense too. Before they perform the rites, they expect to gain knowledge; after performing them they go away deprived even of their expectation.

Col 22

This Column provides an example of the way the Derveni author interprets the Orphic poem. The poem was a theogony, like Hesiod's *Theogony* telling of the birth of the gods and growth of the world. Its details are uncertain, though other Orphic rhapsodies tell of the birth of Protogonos (= Firstborn) from an egg made by Time out of *aither*. In our poem Night may have taken the place of Time; then came the familiar succession of kings, Uranus, Cronus and Zeus, with Zeus gaining power by swallowing (Protogonos, or Uranus' genitals cut off by Cronus). The author says that different deities are in fact one and the same, and explains Demeter's various alternative names by means of some fanciful etymologising.

So (Orpheus) named everything in the same way as best he could, since he understood that people do not all have a similar nature and do not all desire the same things: when they have very great power, they say whatever comes into each of their (5) minds, whatever they happen
5   to want, not at all the same things, driven by greed, sometimes by ignorance too. 'Earth' (*Gē*), 'Mother' (*Mētēr*), 'Rhea' and 'Hera' are all the same. She was called 'Earth' by convention, 'Mother' because everything comes to be from her, 'Ge' and 'Gaia' according to individuals' dialect. She was called (10) 'Demeter' like 'Ge Meter' (*Gē Mētēr*), one name from
10   both, since it was the same. And it is said in the *Hymns* too: 'Demeter, Rhea, Ge, Meter, Hestia, Deio'. For she is called 'Deio' because she was 'damaged' during intercourse; (Orpheus) will make this clear when, according to his verses, she comes to be. She was called 'Rhea' because many (15) animals of all sorts were born [easily] from her. Rhea ...

1–6 Here the author explains why the traditional gods have different names, even though (in his view) they are really one and the same: different people, with different motives, named them differently.

10 *the Hymns*: the author evidently knew other Orphic material. The line quoted gives other names by which Demeter was known, and supports the author's idea that different names can refer to a single divine being. De(i)ō occurs as an alternative for Demeter as early as the *Homeric Hymn to Demeter* 47 (late seventh/early sixth century BC); the identification with Rhea (mother of Zeus) or the Mother (of the Gods) is early fifth century (West 82, n.23, where the identification of Hestia with Earth is also documented; cf. also Betegh 190). Col. 26 seems to identify Demeter/ Rhea with Mind: 'because the Mind is the mother of the other elements'

11–12 *she is called 'Deio' because she was 'damaged' during intercourse*: the author derives 'Deio' from the Greek *dēiō* = 'I ravage'; it is not clear to what story concerning Demeter he is referring.

14 *[easily]*: this supplement is suggested by Janko; the Greek for 'easily' (*Rhaidiōs*) might suggest '*Rhea*'

15. Curse Tablets

Curse tablets, *katadesmoi* ('bindings') in Greek, *defixiones* in Latin, are pieces of lead inscribed with words asking a supernatural power, often a chthonic god such as Hermes or Hecate, to act against someone or something, and often the purpose of these tablets is for an individual to get a personal enemy bound or restrained. More than 1,500 survive from ancient Greece dating from the fifth century BC onwards. Sometimes the tablet was attached to a figurine which might represent the person to be bound. They were often deposited in graves, where the spirits of the dead could readily carry out the instructions inscribed on the tablet, and the act of depositing may have been accompanied by chanting spells and suchlike. The object of the curse is often a rival: athlete, lover, courtroom speaker. The author of the curse rarely reveals his or her name. This could be so the person being cursed would not know on whom to retaliate (Faraone 17), or because the practice was disapproved of (cf. Parker 123). Many later tablets include signs or nonsense words believed to have a supernatural power, and sometimes names are written backwards or with the letters muddled up (see **Text 1** below), or peculiar characters used, perhaps to represent a language intelligible only to the spirits of the dead (Gager 4–12).

Bibliography

C. A. Faraone, 'The Agonistic Context of Early Greek Binding Spells', in *Magika Hiera, Ancient Greek Magic and Religion*, eds C. A. Faraone and D. Obbink (New York and Oxford 1991) 3–32.

J. G. Gager, *Curse Tablets and Binding Spells from the Ancient World* (New York and Oxford 1992).

D. Ogden, *Magic, Witchcraft, and Ghosts in the Greek and Roman Worlds* (Oxford 2002) 210–226.

R. Parker, *Polytheism and Society at Athens* (Oxford 2005) 116–135 (Unlicensed Religion, and Magic).

E. Eidinow, Oracles, *Curses and Risk Among the Ancient Greeks* (Oxford 2007).

1. Eidinow pp. 402–3 = Ziebarth 22
(Side A)

> I consign Zoïs the Eretrian , the wife of Cabeira, to Earth and Hermes – her (5) food, drink, her sleep, laughter, intercourse, her kithara-playing, and her entrance, pleasure, little buttocks, thoughts, eyes .... to Earth

(Side B)

> And to Hermes (I consign) her wicked walk, words, deeds and evil talk ...

This curse tablet, found in Boeotia in 1877 and measuring 8cm × 7cm, is a curse against a man's wife. It is generally thought to have been written by a female rival for the man's affection (so Faraone 14, Gagar 85). The date is uncertain, perhaps 4th century BC.

1 *Eretrian*: from Eretria in Euboea.
Hermes: conductor of souls in the Underworld, *i.e.* 'I wish she were dead'. Hermes is the god most commonly invoked on curse tablets.
2–3 *intercourse ... entrance, pleasure, little buttocks*: explicit sexual references are common on curse tablets. Another one (*IG* 3.3. Appendix ed. Wuensch, 77) says (tr. after Gagar p. 91): (Side A) 'We bind (Callistrate), the wife of Theophemus and Theophilus, son of Callistrate, and the children/slaves of (Calli)strate, both Theophemus and (Eustratus) the brother ... I bind their souls and their deeds and their entire selves and all their belongings. (Side B) and their pricks and their cunts and Cantharis and Dionysius, son of (Cantharis), both themselves and their souls and deeds and all their entire selves and his prick and her unholy cunt'. In this tablet sometimes (denoted by brackets) the names are scrambled with the letters deliberately muddled up in the original Greek ('a symbolic attempt to scramble the persons themselves, rather than an effort to conceal the names from potential human readers' Gagar ad loc.).

2. Eidinow pp. 371–2 = Wuensch 87
(Side A)

     I bind Callias the shopkeeper who is one of my neighbours and his wife Thraitta, and the shop of the bald man and the shop of Anthemion near ... and Philon the shopkeeper: of all of these people I bind the soul, work, hands, feet and their shops. (5) I bind Sosimenes his brother and
5 Carpus his servant, the fabric-seller; and Glycanthis whom they call Malthace; and Agathon the shopkeeper, the servant of Sosimenes: of all of these people I bind the soul, work, life, hands, feet. I bind Cittus my neighbour, the maker of wooden frames, and the skill of Cittus and the work and soul and mind and tongue of Cittus. I bind Mania the lady
10 shopkeeper who is by the spring and the shop of Aristandrus of Eleusis and their work and mind. Soul, hands, tongue, feet, mind: all these I bind in unsealed (?) graves (10) for Hermes the Restrainer.

This is a curse against various shopkeepers (or innkeepers; the Greek word *kapēlos* can mean both). It is not clear why the curse is made ('competition between small-scale merchants' Gager 156; perhaps a customer had been swindled, Ogden 215). It is one of a number of curse tablets denouncing owners of small businesses. It is Attic, 4th century BC.

8 *the maker of wooden frames*: or perhaps 'rope-maker'
11–12 *I bind in unsealed (?) graves for Hermes the Restrainer*: the curse tablet was probably put in a grave that had been surreptitiously opened, with a view to Hermes (in his capacity as *psychopompos* or 'conductor of souls') binding and

restraining the cursed people and taking them away to the Underworld. The tablets were commonly put in graves, as they provided a ready link to the infernal powers who were to carry out the curse.

3. Eidinow pp. 427–8 = Dubois 37 (L. Dubois, Inscriptions Grecques Dialectales de Sicile (Rome 1989))
(Side A)
> I indict the man from Selinous and the tongue of the man from Selinous so that it is twisted to be useless for them. (5) And I indict the tongues of the foreigners involved in the trial so that they are twisted to be useless for them.

(Side B)
> I indict Timaso and the tongue of Timaso so that it is twisted to be useless for them. I indict the Tyrrhenian woman and the tongue of the Tyrrhenian woman so that it is twisted to be useless for all of them.

This is one of the earliest Greek curse tablets, probably early fifth century BC. It was found in a sanctuary of Demeter Malophoros at Selinous, a Greek colony in Sicily, and is a somewhat unusual round tablet *c.* 4.3cm in diameter (illustrations Dubois 48, Gager 141). It belongs to a type probably written by a defendant before a trial: 'They are attempts at binding the opponent's ability to think clearly and speak effectively in court in the hope that a dismal performance will cause him to lose the case', Faraone 15.

(Side A)
1 *tongue*: the relevant part of the body to be cursed in a judicial case involving speakers, just as it was the hands and feet that were cursed in the case involving shopkeepers above.
2 *twisted to be useless*: *i.e.* so that he is tongue-tied.
them: his party in the dispute.
3 *foreigners involved in the trial*: perhaps, but not necessarily, witnesses. Being a colony Selinous attracted foreigners, and the case may have concerned legality of citizenship.

(Side B)
1–2 *Timaso ... the Tyrrhenian woman*: Timaso is a woman's name. It is noteworthy that women are mentioned as involved in giving oral evidence at the trial: in Athens women were excluded from giving testimony.
Tyrrhenian: from Etruria, central Italy.

GREEK TEXTS

1. Homer *Iliad* 1.188–222

The text is based on the *Oxford Classical Text* eds D. B. Monro and T. W. Allen (Oxford 1902).

'Ὣς φάτο· Πηλεΐωνι δ' ἄχος γένετ', ἐν δέ οἱ ἦτορ
στήθεσσιν λασίοισι διάνδιχα μερμήριξεν,
ἢ ὅ γε φάσγανον ὀξὺ ἐρυσσάμενος παρὰ μηροῦ   190
τοὺς μὲν ἀναστήσειεν, ὃ δ' Ἀτρεΐδην ἐναρίζοι,
ἦε χόλον παύσειεν ἐρητύσειέ τε θυμόν.
ἧος ὃ ταῦθ' ὥρμαινε κατὰ φρένα καὶ κατὰ θυμόν,
ἕλκετο δ' ἐκ κολεοῖο μέγα ξίφος, ἦλθε δ' Ἀθήνη
οὐρανόθεν· πρὸ γὰρ ἦκε θεὰ λευκώλενος Ἥρη,   195
ἄμφω ὁμῶς θυμῷ φιλέουσά τε κηδομένη τε·
στῆ δ' ὄπιθεν, ξανθῆς δὲ κόμης ἕλε Πηλεΐωνα
οἴῳ φαινομένη· τῶν δ' ἄλλων οὔ τις ὁρᾶτο·
θάμβησεν δ' Ἀχιλεύς, μετὰ δ' ἐτράπετ', αὐτίκα δ' ἔγνω
Παλλάδ' Ἀθηναίην· δεινὼ δέ οἱ ὄσσε φάανθεν·   200
καί μιν φωνήσας ἔπεα πτερόεντα προσηύδα·
"τίπτ' αὖτ' αἰγιόχοιο Διὸς τέκος εἰλήλουθας;
ἦ ἵνα ὕβριν ἴδῃ Ἀγαμέμνονος Ἀτρεΐδαο;
ἀλλ' ἔκ τοι ἐρέω, τὸ δὲ καὶ τελέεσθαι ὀίω·
ἧς ὑπεροπλίῃσι τάχ' ἄν ποτε θυμὸν ὀλέσσῃ."   205
Τὸν δ' αὖτε προσέειπε θεὰ γλαυκῶπις Ἀθήνη·
"ἦλθον ἐγὼ παύσουσα τὸ σὸν μένος, αἴ κε πίθηαι,
οὐρανόθεν· πρὸ δέ μ' ἦκε θεὰ λευκώλενος Ἥρη,
ἄμφω ὁμῶς θυμῷ φιλέουσά τε κηδομένη τε·
ἀλλ' ἄγε λῆγ' ἔριδος, μηδὲ ξίφος ἕλκεο χειρί·   210
ἀλλ' ἤτοι ἔπεσιν μὲν ὀνείδισον ὡς ἔσεταί περ·
ὧδε γὰρ ἐξερέω, τὸ δὲ καὶ τετελεσμένον ἔσται·
καί ποτέ τοι τρὶς τόσσα παρέσσεται ἀγλαὰ δῶρα
ὕβριος εἵνεκα τῆσδε· σὺ δ' ἴσχεο, πείθεο δ' ἡμῖν."
Τὴν δ' ἀπαμειβόμενος προσέφη πόδας ὠκὺς Ἀχιλεύς·   215
"χρὴ μὲν σφωΐτερόν γε θεὰ ἔπος εἰρύσσασθαι
καὶ μάλα περ θυμῷ κεχολωμένον· ὡς γὰρ ἄμεινον·
ὅς κε θεοῖς ἐπιπείθηται μάλα τ' ἔκλυον αὐτοῦ"

Ἦ καὶ ἐπ' ἀργυρέῃ κώπῃ σχέθε χεῖρα βαρεῖαν,
ἂψ δ' ἐς κουλεὸν ὦσε μέγα ξίφος, οὐδ' ἀπίθησε   220
μύθῳ Ἀθηναίης· ἣ δ' Οὔλυμπόνδε βεβήκει
δώματ' ἐς αἰγιόχοιο Διὸς μετὰ δαίμονας ἄλλους.

2. Hesiod *Works and Days* 724–828

The text is based on the edition of the *Works and Days* by M. L. West (Oxford 1978).

μηδέ ποτ' ἐξ ἠοῦς Διὶ λείβειν αἴθοπα οἶνον
χερσὶν ἀνίπτοισιν μηδ' ἄλλοις ἀθανάτοισιν·   725
οὐ γὰρ τοί γε κλύουσιν, ἀποπτύουσι δέ τ' ἀράς.
μηδ' ἄντ' ἠελίου τετραμμένος ὀρθὸς ὀμείχειν,
αὐτὰρ ἐπεί κε δύῃ, μεμνημένος, ἔς τ' ἀνιόντα,
μήτ' ἐν ὁδῷ μήτ' ἐκτὸς ὁδοῦ προβάδην οὐρήσῃς·
μηδ' ἀπογυμνωθείς· μακάρων τοι νύκτες ἔασιν.   730
ἑζόμενος δ' ὅ γε θεῖος ἀνήρ, πεπνυμένα εἰδώς,
ἢ ὅ γε πρὸς τοῖχον πελάσας εὐερκέος αὐλῆς.
μηδ' αἰδοῖα γονῇ πεπαλαγμένος ἔνδοθι οἴκου
ἱστίῃ ἐμπελαδὸν παραφαινέμεν, ἀλλ' ἀλέασθαι.
μηδ' ἀπὸ δυσφήμοιο τάφου ἀπονοστήσαντα   735
σπερμαίνειν γενεήν, ἀλλ' ἀθανάτων ἀπὸ δαιτός.
μηδέ ποτ' ἐν προχοῇς ποταμῶν ἅλαδε προρεόντων   757
μηδ' ἐπὶ κρηνάων οὐρεῖν, μάλα δ' ἐξαλέασθαι·   758
μηδ' ἐναποψύχειν· τὸ γὰρ οὔ τοι λώιόν ἐστιν.   759
μηδέ ποτ' ἀενάων ποταμῶν καλλίρροον ὕδωρ   737
ποσσὶ περᾶν πρίν γ' εὔξῃ ἰδὼν ἐς καλὰ ῥέεθρα
χεῖρας νιψάμενος πολυηράτῳ ὕδατι λευκῷ.
ὃς ποταμὸν διαβῇ κακότητ' ἰδὲ χεῖρας ἄνιπτος,   740
τῷ δὲ θεοὶ νεμεσῶσι καὶ ἄλγεα δῶκαν ὀπίσσω.
μηδ' ἀπὸ πεντόζοιο θεῶν ἐν δαιτὶ θαλείῃ
αὖον ἀπὸ χλωροῦ τάμνειν αἴθωνι σιδήρῳ.
μηδέ ποτ' οἰνοχόην τιθέμεν κρητῆρος ὕπερθεν
πινόντων· ὀλοὴ γὰρ ἐπ' αὐτῷ μοῖρα τέτυκται.   745
μηδὲ δόμον ποιῶν ἀνεπίξεστον καταλείπειν,
μή τοι ἐφεζομένη κρώξῃ λακέρυζα κορώνη.
μηδ' ἀπὸ χυτροπόδων ἀνεπιρρέκτων ἀνελόντα
ἔσθειν μηδὲ λόεσθαι· ἐπεὶ καὶ τοῖς ἔπι ποινή.

μηδ᾽ ἐπ᾽ ἀκινήτοισι καθίζειν, οὐ γὰρ ἄμεινον,   750
παῖδα δυωδεκαταῖον, ὅ τ᾽ ἀνέρ᾽ ἀνήνορα ποιεῖ,
μηδὲ δυωδεκάμηνον· ἴσον καὶ τοῦτο τέτυκται.
μηδὲ γυναικείῳ λουτρῷ χρόα φαιδρύνεσθαι
ἀνέρα· λευγαλέη γὰρ ἐπὶ χρόνον ἔστ᾽ ἐπὶ καὶ τῷ
ποινή. μηδ᾽ ἱεροῖσιν ἐπ᾽ αἰθομένοισι κυρήσας   755
μωμεύειν ἀίδηλα· θεός νύ τι καὶ τὰ νεμεσσᾷ.   756
ὧδ᾽ ἔρδειν· δεινὴν δὲ βροτῶν ὑπαλεύεο φήμην·   760
φήμη γάρ τε κακὴ πέλεται κούφη μὲν ἀεῖραι
ῥεῖα μάλ᾽, ἀργαλέη δὲ φέρειν, χαλεπὴ δ᾽ ἀποθέσθαι.
φήμη δ᾽ οὔ τις πάμπαν ἀπόλλυται, ἥντινα πολλοὶ
λαοὶ φημίξουσι· θεός νύ τίς ἐστι καὶ αὐτή.

ἤματα δ᾽ ἐκ Διόθεν πεφυλαγμένος εὖ κατὰ μοῖραν   765
πεφραδέμεν δμώεσσι· τριηκάδα μηνὸς ἀρίστην
ἔργα τ᾽ ἐποπτεύειν ἠδ᾽ ἁρμαλιὴν δατέασθαι,
εὖτ᾽ ἂν ἀληθείην λαοὶ κρίνοντες ἄγωσιν.
αἵδε γὰρ ἡμέραι εἰσὶ Διὸς παρὰ μητιόεντος·
πρῶτον ἔνη τετράς τε καὶ ἑβδόμη ἱερὸν ἦμαρ·   770
(τῇ γὰρ Ἀπόλλωνα χρυσάορα γείνατο Λητώ)
ὀγδοάτη τ᾽ ἐνάτη τε. δύω γε μὲν ἤματα μηνὸς
ἔξοχ᾽ ἀεξομένοιο βροτήσια ἔργα πένεσθαι,
ἑνδεκάτη τε δυωδεκάτη τ᾽· ἄμφω γε μὲν ἐσθλαί,
ἠμὲν ὄις πείκειν ἠδ᾽ εὔφρονα καρπὸν ἀμᾶσθαι,   775
ἡ δὲ δυωδεκάτη τῆς ἑνδεκάτης μέγ᾽ ἀμείνων·
τῇ γάρ τοι νῇ νήματ᾽ ἀερσιπότητος ἀράχνης
ἤματος ἐκ πλείου, ὅτε τ᾽ ἴδρις σωρὸν ἀμᾶται·
τῇ δ᾽ ἱστὸν στήσαιτο γυνὴ προβάλοιτό τε ἔργον.
μηνὸς δ᾽ ἱσταμένου τρεισκαιδεκάτην ἀλέασθαι   780
σπέρματος ἄρξασθαι· φυτὰ δ᾽ ἐνθρέψασθαι ἀρίστη.
ἕκτη δ᾽ ἡ μέσση μάλ᾽ ἀσύμφορός ἐστι φυτοῖσιν,
ἀνδρογόνος δ᾽ ἀγαθή· κούρῃ δ᾽ οὐ σύμφορός ἐστιν
οὔτε γενέσθαι πρῶτ᾽ οὔτ᾽ ἂρ γάμου ἀντιβολῆσαι.
οὐδὲ μὲν ἡ πρώτη ἕκτη κούρῃ γε γενέσθαι   785
ἄρμενος, ἀλλ᾽ ἐρίφους τάμνειν καὶ πώεα μήλων,
σηκόν τ᾽ ἀμφιβαλεῖν ποιμνήιον ἤπιον ἦμαρ·
ἐσθλὴ δ᾽ ἀνδρογόνος· φιλέοι δέ κε κέρτομα βάζειν
ψεύδεά θ᾽ αἱμυλίους τε λόγους κρυφίους τ᾽ ὀαρισμούς.
μηνὸς δ᾽ ὀγδοάτῃ κάπρον καὶ βοῦν ἐρίμυκον   790

ταμνέμεν, οὐρῆας δὲ δυωδεκάτῃ ταλαεργούς.
εἰκάδι δ' ἐν μεγάλῃ πλέῳ ἤματι ἵστορα φῶτα
γείνασθαι· μάλα γάρ τε νόον πεπυκασμένος ἔσται.
ἐσθλὴ δ' ἀνδρογόνος δεκάτη, κούρῃ δέ τε τετρὰς
μέσσῃ· τῇ δέ τε μῆλα καὶ εἰλίποδας ἕλικας βοῦς   795
καὶ κύνα καρχαρόδοντα καὶ οὐρῆας ταλαεργοὺς
πρηΰνειν ἐπὶ χεῖρα τιθείς· πεφύλαξο δὲ θυμῷ
τετράδ' ἀλεύασθαι φθίνοντός θ' ἱσταμένου τε
ἄλγεσι θυμοβορεῖν· μάλα τοι τετελεσμένον ἦμαρ.
ἐν δὲ τετάρτῃ μηνὸς ἄγεσθ' εἰς οἶκον ἄκοιτιν,   800
οἰωνοὺς κρίνας οἳ ἐπ' ἔργματι τούτῳ ἄριστοι.
πέμπτας δ' ἐξαλέασθαι, ἐπεὶ χαλεπαί τε καὶ αἰναί·
ἐν πέμπτῃ γάρ φασιν Ἐρινύας ἀμφιπολεύειν
Ὅρκον γεινόμενον, τὸν Ἔρις τέκε πῆμ' ἐπιόρκοις.
μέσσῃ δ' ἑβδομάτῃ Δήμητερος ἱερὸν ἀκτὴν   805
εὖ μάλ' ὀπιπεύοντα ἐυτροχάλῳ ἐν ἀλωῇ
βάλλειν, ὑλοτόμον τε ταμεῖν θαλαμήια δοῦρα
νήιά τε ξύλα πολλά, τά τ' ἄρμενα νηυσὶ πέλονται.
τετράδι δ' ἄρχεσθαι νῆας πήγνυσθαι ἀραιάς.
εἰνὰς δ' ἡ μέσση ἐπὶ δείελα λώιον ἦμαρ·   810
πρωτίστη δ' εἰνὰς παναπήμων ἀνθρώποισιν·
ἐσθλὴ μὲν γάρ θ' ἥ γε φυτευέμεν ἠδὲ γενέσθαι
ἀνέρι τ' ἠδὲ γυναικί, καὶ οὔποτε πάγκακον ἦμαρ.
παῦροι δ' αὖτε ἴσασι τρισεινάδα μηνὸς ἀρίστην
ἄρξασθαί τε πίθου καὶ ἐπὶ ζυγὸν αὐχένι θεῖναι   815
βουσὶ καὶ ἡμιόνοισι καὶ ἵπποις ὠκυπόδεσσι,
νέα <τε> πολυκλήιδα θοὴν εἰς οἴνοπα πόντον
εἰρύμεναι· παῦροι δέ τ' ἀληθέα κικλήσκουσιν.
τετράδι δ' οἴγε πίθον – περὶ πάντων ἱερὸν ἦμαρ –
μέσσῃ. παῦροι δ' αὖτε μετεικάδα μηνὸς ἀρίστην   820
ἠοῦς γεινομένης· ἐπὶ δείελα δ' ἐστὶ χερείων.
αἵδε μὲν ἡμέραι εἰσὶν ἐπιχθονίοις μέγ' ὄνειαρ·
αἱ δ' ἄλλαι μετάδουποι, ἀκήριοι, οὔ τι φέρουσαι,
ἄλλος δ' ἀλλοίην αἰνεῖ, παῦροι δὲ ἴσασιν·
ἄλλοτε μητρυιὴ πέλει ἡμέρη, ἄλλοτε μήτηρ   825
τάων. εὐδαίμων τε καὶ ὄλβιος, ὃς τάδε πάντα
εἰδὼς ἐργάζεται ἀναίτιος ἀθανάτοισιν,
ὄρνιθας κρίνων καὶ ὑπερβασίας ἀλεείνων.

3. Theophrastus, *Characters* 16

The text is based on the *Oxford Classical Text* ed. H. Diels (Oxford 1909).

ΔΕΙΣΙΔΑΙΜΟΝΙΑΣ

Ἀμέλει ἡ δεισιδαιμονία δόξειεν <ἂν> εἶναι δειλία πρὸς
τὸ δαιμόνιον, ὁ δὲ δεισιδαίμων τοιοῦτός τις, οἷος ἐπὶ κρήνῃ
ἀπονιψάμενος τὰς χεῖρας καὶ περιρρανάμενος ἀπὸ ἱεροῦ
δάφνην εἰς τὸ στόμα λαβὼν οὕτω τὴν ἡμέραν περιπατεῖν.   5
καὶ τὴν ὁδὸν ἐὰν ὑπερδράμῃ γαλῆ, μὴ πρότερον πορευθῆναι,
ἕως διεξέλθῃ τις ἢ λίθους τρεῖς ὑπὲρ τῆς ὁδοῦ διαβάλῃ.
καὶ ἐὰν ἴδῃ ὄφιν ἐν τῇ οἰκίᾳ, ἐὰν παρείαν, Σαβάζιον καλεῖν,
ἐὰν δὲ ἱερόν, ἐνταῦθα ἡρῷον εὐθὺς ἱδρύσασθαι. καὶ τῶν
λιπαρῶν λίθων τῶν ἐν ταῖς τριόδοις παριὼν ἐκ τῆς ληκύθου   10
ἔλαιον καταχεῖν καὶ ἐπὶ γόνατα πεσὼν καὶ προσκυνήσας
ἀπαλλάττεσθαι. καὶ ἐὰν μῦς θύλακον ἀλφίτων διαφάγῃ,
πρὸς τὸν ἐξηγητὴν ἐλθὼν ἐρωτᾶν, τί χρὴ ποιεῖν, καὶ ἐὰν
ἀποκρίνηται αὐτῷ ἐκδοῦναι τῷ σκυτοδέψῃ ἐπιρράψαι, μὴ
προσέχειν τούτοις, ἀλλ᾽ ἀποτραπεὶς ἐκθύσασθαι. καὶ πυκνὰ   15
δὲ τὴν οἰκίαν καθᾶραι δεινὸς Ἑκάτης φάσκων ἐπαγωγὴν
γεγονέναι. κἂν γλαῦκες βαδίζοντος αὐτοῦ <ἀνακράγωσι>,
ταράττεσθαι καὶ εἴπας· Ἀθηνᾶ κρείττων, παρελθεῖν οὕτω.
καὶ οὔτε ἐπιβῆναι μνήματι οὔτ᾽ ἐπὶ νεκρὸν οὔτ᾽ ἐπὶ λεχὼ
ἐλθεῖν ἐθελῆσαι, ἀλλὰ τὸ μὴ μιαίνεσθαι συμφέρον αὐτῷ   20
φῆσαι εἶναι. καὶ ταῖς τετράσι δὲ καὶ ἑβδομάσι προσ-
τάξας οἶνον ἕψειν τοῖς ἔνδον, ἐξελθὼν ἀγοράσαι μυρρίνας,
λιβανωτόν, πόπανα καὶ εἰσελθὼν εἴσω στεφανοῦν τους
Ἑρμαφροδίτους ὅλην τὴν ἡμέραν. καὶ ὅταν ἐνύπνιον ἴδῃ,
πορεύεσθαι πρὸς τοὺς ὀνειροκρίτας, πρὸς τοὺς μάντεις, πρὸς 25
τοὺς ὀρνιθοσκόπους, ἐρωτήσων, τίνι θεῶν ἢ θεᾷ εὔχεσθαι
δεῖ. καὶ τελεσθησόμενος πρὸς τοὺς Ὀρφεοτελεστὰς κατὰ
μῆνα πορεύεσθαι μετὰ τῆς γυναικός (ἐὰν δὲ μὴ σχολάζῃ
ἡ γυνή, μετὰ τῆς τίτθης) καὶ τῶν παιδίων. καὶ τῶν
περιρραινομένων ἐπὶ θαλάττης ἐπιμελῶς δόξειεν ἂν εἶναι.   30
κἄν ποτε ἐπίδῃ σκορόδῳ ἐστεμμένον τῶν ἐπὶ ταῖς τριόδοις,
ἀπελθὼν κατὰ κεφαλῆς λούσασθαι καὶ ἱερείας καλέσας
σκίλλῃ ἢ σκύλακι κελεῦσαι αὐτὸν περικαθᾶραι. μαινόμενον
δὲ ἰδὼν ἢ ἐπίληπτον φρίξας εἰς κόλπον πτύσαι.

4. Herodotus 6. 105–106: A Divine Epiphany (Pheidippides and Pan)

The text is based on the *Oxford Classical Text*³ ed. C. Hude (Oxford 1926).

105
Καὶ πρῶτα μὲν ἐόντες ἔτι ἐν τῷ ἄστεϊ οἱ στρατηγοὶ
ἀποπέμπουσι ἐς Σπάρτην κήρυκα Φειδιππίδην, Ἀθηναῖον
μὲν ἄνδρα, ἄλλως δὲ ἡμεροδρόμην τε καὶ τοῦτο μελετῶντα.
τῷ δή, ὡς αὐτός τε ἔλεγε Φειδιππίδης καὶ Ἀθηναίοισι
ἀπήγγελλε, περὶ τὸ Παρθένιον ὄρος τὸ ὑπὲρ Τεγέης ὁ
Πὰν περιπίπτει. βώσαντα δὲ τὸ οὔνομα τοῦ Φειδιππίδεω
τὸν Πᾶνα Ἀθηναίοισι κελεῦσαι ἀπαγγεῖλαι δι' ὅ τι ἑωυτοῦ
οὐδεμίαν ἐπιμελείην ποιεῦνται, ἐόντος εὐνόου Ἀθηναίοισι
καὶ πολλαχῇ γενομένου σφι ἤδη χρησίμου, τὰ δ' ἔτι καὶ
ἐσομένου. καὶ ταῦτα μὲν Ἀθηναῖοι, καταστάντων σφι
εὖ τῶν πρηγμάτων, πιστεύσαντες εἶναι ἀληθέα ἱδρύ-
σαντο ὑπὸ τῇ Ἀκροπόλι Πανὸς ἱρόν, καὶ αὐτὸν ἀπὸ ταύτης
τῆς ἀγγελίης θυσίῃσί τε ἐπετείοισι καὶ λαμπάδι ἱλάσκονται.

106
τότε δὲ πεμφθεὶς ὑπὸ τῶν στρατηγῶν ὁ Φειδιππίδης
οὗτος, ὅτε πέρ οἱ ἔφη καὶ τὸν Πᾶνα φανῆναι, δευτεραῖος
ἐκ τοῦ Ἀθηναίων ἄστεος ἦν ἐν Σπάρτῃ, ἀπικόμενος δὲ
ἐπὶ τοὺς ἄρχοντας ἔλεγε· Ὦ Λακεδαιμόνιοι, Ἀθηναῖοι
ὑμέων δέονται σφίσι βοηθῆσαι καὶ μὴ περιιδεῖν πόλιν
ἀρχαιοτάτην ἐν τοῖσι Ἕλλησι δουλοσύνῃ περιπεσοῦσαν
πρὸς ἀνδρῶν βαρβάρων. καὶ γὰρ νῦν Ἐρέτριά τε ἠνδρα-
πόδισται καὶ πόλι λογίμῳ ἡ Ἑλλὰς γέγονε ἀσθενεστέρη.
ὁ μὲν δή σφι τὰ ἐντεταλμένα ἀπήγγελλε, τοῖσι δὲ ἔαδε
μὲν βοηθέειν Ἀθηναίοισι, ἀδύνατα δέ σφι ἦν τὸ παραυ-
τίκα ποιεῖν ταῦτα οὐ βουλομένοισι λύειν τὸν νόμον· ἦν
γὰρ ἱσταμένου τοῦ μηνὸς εἰνάτη, εἰνάτη δὲ οὐκ ἐξελεύ-
σεσθαι ἔφασαν μὴ οὐ πλήρεος ἐόντος τοῦ κύκλου.

5. Aeschylus *Agamemnon* 160–184: Hymn to Zeus
The text is based on the Teubner edition ed. M. L. West (Leipzig 1990).

Ζεύς, ὅστις ποτ' ἐστίν, εἰ τόδ' αὐτῷ φίλον κεκλημένῳ,
τοῦτό νιν προσεννέπω.
οὐκ ἔχω προσεικάσαι
πάντ' ἐπισταθμώμενος
πλὴν Διός, εἰ τὸ μάταν ἀπὸ φροντίδος ἄχθος   165
χρὴ βαλεῖν ἐτητύμως.

οὔθ' ὅστις πάροιθεν ἦν μέγας
παμμάχῳ θράσει βρύων,
οὐδὲ λέξ<ετ>αι πρὶν ὤν·   170
ὅς τ' ἔπειτ' ἔφυ, τριακ-
τῆρος οἴχεται τυχών·
Ζῆνα δέ τις προφρόνως ἐπινίκια κλάζων
τεύξεται φρενῶν τὸ πᾶν,   175

τὸν φρονεῖν βροτοὺς ὁδώ-
σαντα, τὸν πάθει μάθος
θέντα κυρίως ἔχειν.
στάζει δ' ἀνθ' ὕπνου πρὸ καρδίας
μνησιπήμων πόνος· καὶ παρ' ἄ-   180
κοντας ἦλθε σωφρονεῖν.
δαιμόνων δέ που χάρις
βίαιος σέλμα σεμνὸν ἡμένων.

6. The victorious athlete
Pindar, *Pythian* 10. The text is based on the Teubner edition eds B. Snell and
H. Maehler[8] (Leipzig 1987).

Α΄ Ὀλβία Λακεδαίμων,
μάκαιρα Θεσσαλία. πατρὸς δ' ἀμφοτέραις ἐξ ἑνός
ἀριστομάχου γένος Ἡρακλέος βασιλεύει.
τί κομπέω παρὰ καιρόν; ἀλλά με Πυθώ
τε καὶ τὸ Πελινναῖον ἀπύει
Ἀλεύα τε παῖδες, Ἱπποκλέα θέλοντες   5

ἀγαγεῖν ἐπικωμίαν ἀνδρῶν κλυτὰν ὄπα.
γεύεται γὰρ ἀέθλων·
στρατῷ τ᾽ ἀμφικτιόνων ὁ Παρνάσσιος αὐτὸν μυχός
διαυλοδρομᾶν ὕπατον παίδων ἀνέειπεν.
Ἄπολλον, γλυκὺ δ᾽ ἀνθρώπων τέλος ἀρχά   10
    τε δαίμονος ὀρνύντος αὔξεται·
ὁ μέν που τεοῖς τε μήδεσι τοῦτ᾽ ἔπραξεν,
τὸ δὲ συγγενὲς ἐμβέβακεν ἴχνεσιν πατρός
Ὀλυμπιονίκα δὶς ἐν πολεμαδόκοις
Ἄρεος ὅπλοις·
ἔθηκε καὶ βαθυλείμων ὑπὸ Κίρρας πετρᾶν   15
ἀγὼν κρατησίποδα Φρικίαν.
ἕποιτο μοῖρα καὶ ὑστέραισιν
ἐν ἁμέραις ἀγάνορα πλοῦτον ἀνθεῖν σφίσιν·

Β΄ τῶν δ᾽ ἐν Ἑλλάδι τερπνῶν
λαχόντες οὐκ ὀλίγαν δόσιν, μὴ φθονεραῖς ἐκ θεῶν   20
μετατροπίαις ἐπικύρσαιεν. θεὸς εἴη
ἀπήμων κέαρ· εὐδαίμων δὲ καὶ ὑμνη-
    τὸς οὗτος ἀνὴρ γίνεται σοφοῖς,
ὃς ἂν χερσὶν ἢ ποδῶν ἀρετᾷ κρατήσαις
τὰ μέγιστ᾽ ἀέθλων ἕλῃ τόλμᾳ τε καὶ σθένει,
καὶ ζώων ἔτι νεαρόν   25
κατ᾽ αἶσαν υἱὸν ἴδῃ τυχόντα στεφάνων Πυθίων.
ὁ χάλκεος οὐρανὸς οὔ ποτ᾽ ἀμβατὸς αὐτῷ·
ὅσαις δὲ βροτὸν ἔθνος ἀγλαΐαις ἁ-
    πτόμεσθα, περαίνει πρὸς ἔσχατον
πλόον· ναυσὶ δ᾽ οὔτε πεζὸς ἰών <κεν> εὕροις
ἐς Ὑπερβορέων ἀγῶνα θαυμαστὰν ὁδόν.   30
παρ᾽ οἷς ποτε Περσεὺς ἐδαίσατο λαγέτας,
δώματ᾽ ἐσελθών,
κλειτὰς ὄνων ἑκατόμβας ἐπιτόσσαις θεῷ
ῥέζοντας· ὧν θαλίαις ἔμπεδον
εὐφαμίαις τε μάλιστ᾽ Ἀπόλλων   35
χαίρει, γελᾷ θ᾽ ὁρῶν ὕβριν ὀρθίαν κνωδάλων.

Γ΄ Μοῖσα δ᾽ οὐκ ἀποδαμεῖ
τρόποις ἐπὶ σφετέροισι· παντᾷ δὲ χοροὶ παρθένων
λυρᾶν τε βοαὶ καναχαί τ᾽ αὐλῶν δονέονται·

δάφνᾳ τε χρυσέᾳ κόμας ἀναδήσαν-   40
τες εἰλαπινάζοισιν εὐφρόνως.
νόσοι δ' οὔτε γῆρας οὐλόμενον κέκραται
ἱερᾷ γενεᾷ· πόνων δὲ καὶ μαχᾶν ἄτερ
οἰκέοισι φυγόντες
ὑπέρδικον Νέμεσιν. θρασείᾳ δὲ πνέων καρδίᾳ
μόλεν Δανάας ποτὲ παῖς, ἀγεῖτο δ' Ἀθάνα,   45
ἐς ἀνδρῶν μακάρων ὅμιλον· ἔπεφνέν
τε Γοργόνα, καὶ ποικίλον κάρα
δρακόντων φόβαισιν ἤλυθε νασιώταις
λίθινον θάνατον φέρων. ἐμοὶ δὲ θαυμάσαι
θεῶν τελεσάντων οὐδέν ποτε φαίνεται
ἔμμεν ἄπιστον.   50
κώπαν σχάσον, ταχὺ δ' ἄγκυραν ἔρεισον χθονί
πρῴραθε, χοιράδος ἄλκαρ πέτρας.
ἐγκωμίων γὰρ ἄωτος ὕμνων
ἐπ' ἄλλοτ' ἄλλον ὧτε μέλισσα θύνει λόγον.

Δ΄ ἔλπομαι δ' Ἐφυραίων   55
ὄπ' ἀμφὶ Πηνεϊὸν γλυκεῖαν προχεόντων ἐμάν
τὸν Ἱπποκλέαν ἔτι καὶ μᾶλλον σὺν ἀοιδαῖς
ἕκατι στεφάνων θαητὸν ἐν ἅλι-
   ξι θησέμεν ἐν καὶ παλαιτέροις,
νέαισίν τε παρθένοισι μέλημα. καὶ γάρ
ἑτέροις ἑτέρων ἔρωτες ἔκνιξαν φρένας·   60
τῶν δ' ἕκαστος ὀρούει,
τυχών κεν ἁρπαλέαν σχέθοι φροντίδα τὰν πὰρ ποδός·
τὰ δ' εἰς ἐνιαυτὸν ἀτέκμαρτον προνοῆσαι.
πέποιθα ξενίᾳ προσανεῖ Θώρα-
   κος, ὅσπερ ἐμὰν ποιπνύων χάριν
τόδ' ἔζευξεν ἅρμα Πιερίδων τετράορον,   65
φιλέων φιλέοντ', ἄγων ἄγοντα προφρόνως.
πειρῶντι δὲ καὶ χρυσὸς ἐν βασάνῳ πρέπει
καὶ νόος ὀρθός.
ἀδελφεοῖσί τ' ἐπαινήσομεν ἐσλοῖς, ὅτι
ὑψοῦ φέροντι νόμον Θεσσαλῶν   70
αὔξοντες· ἐν δ' ἀγαθοῖσι κεῖται
πατρώϊαι κεδναὶ πολίων κυβερνάσιες.

7. Empedocles, Selected Fragments

The text is based on H. Diels and W. Kranz, *Fragmente der Vorsokratiker*[10] (Berlin 1952).

115

ἔστιν Ἀνάγκης χρῆμα, θεῶν ψήφισμα παλαιόν,
ἀίδιον, πλατέεσσι κατεσφρηγισμένον ὅρκοις·
εὖτέ τις ἀμπλακίηισι φόνωι φίλα γυῖα μιήνηι,
<νείκεΐ θ'> ὅς κ(ε) ἐπίορκον ἁμαρτήσας ἐπομόσσηι,
δαίμονες οἵτε μακραίωνος λελάχασι βίοιο,   5
τρίς μιν μυρίας ὥρας ἀπὸ μακάρων ἀλάλησθαι,
φυομένους παντοῖα διὰ χρόνου εἴδεα θνητῶν
ἀργαλέας βιότοιο μεταλλάσσοντα κελεύθους.
αἰθέριον μὲν γάρ σφε μένος πόντονδε διώκει,
πόντος δ' ἐς χθονὸς οὖδας ἀπέπτυσε, γαῖα δ' ἐς αὐγὰς   10
ἠελίου φαέθοντος, ὁ δ' αἰθέρος ἔμβαλε δίναις·
ἄλλος δ' ἐξ ἄλλου δέχεται, στυγέουσι δὲ πάντες.
τῶν καὶ ἐγὼ νῦν εἰμι, φυγὰς θεόθεν καὶ ἀλήτης,
νείκεΐ μαινομένωι πίσυνος.

117

Ἤδη γάρ ποτ' ἐγὼ γενόμην κοῦρός τε κόρη τε
θάμνος τ' οἰωνός τε καὶ ἔξαλος ἔλλοπος ἰχθῦς.

112

ὦ φίλοι, οἳ μέγα ἄστυ κατὰ ξανθοῦ Ἀκράγαντος
ναίετ' ἀν' ἄκρα πόλεος, ἀγαθῶν μελεδήμονες ἔργων,
ξείνων αἰδοῖοι λιμένες, κακότητος ἄπειροι,
χαίρετ'· ἐγὼ δ' ὑμῖν θεὸς ἄμβροτος, οὐκέτι θνητός
πωλεῦμαι μετὰ πᾶσι τετιμένος, ὥσπερ ἔοικα,   5
ταινίαις τε περίστεπτος στέφεσίν τε θαλείοις.
τοῖσιν † ἄμ' † ἂν ἵκωμαι ἄστεα τηλεθάοντα,
ἀνδράσιν ἠδὲ γυναιξί, σεβίζομαι· οἱ δ' ἄμ' ἕπονται
μυρίοι ἐξερέοντες, ὅπηι πρὸς κέρδος ἀταρπός,
οἱ μὲν μαντοσυνέων κεχρημένοι, οἱ δ' ἐπὶ νούσων   10
παντοίων ἐπύθοντο κλυεῖν εὐηκέα βάξιν,
δηρὸν δὴ χαλεπῆισι πεπαρμένοι <ἀμφ' ὀδύνηισιν>.

127
ἐν θήρεσσι λέοντες ὀρειλεχέες χαμαιεῦναι
γίγνονται, δάφναι δ' ἐνὶ δένδρεσιν ἠυκόμοισιν.

146
εἰς δὲ τέλος μάντεις τε καὶ ὑμνοπόλοι καὶ ἰητροί
καὶ πρόμοι ἀνθρώποισιν ἐπιχθονίοισι πέλονται,
ἔνθεν ἀναβλαστοῦσι θεοὶ τιμῆισι φέριστοι.

147
ἀθανάτοις ἄλλοισιν ὁμέστιοι, αὐτοτράπεζοι
ἐόντες, ἀνδρείων ἀχέων ἀπόκληροι, ἀτειρεῖς.

130
ἦσαν δὲ κτίλα πάντα καὶ ἀνθρώποισι προσηνῆ,
θῆρές τ' οἰωνοί τε, φιλοφροσύνη τε δεδήει.

135
ἀλλὰ τὸ μὲν πάντων νόμιμον διά τ' εὐρυμέδοντος
αἰθέρος ἠνεκέως τέταται διά τ' ἀπλέτου αὐγῆς.

139
οἴμοι ὅτι οὐ πρόσθεν με διώλεσε νηλεὲς ἦμαρ,
πρὶν χηλαῖς σχέτλι' ἔργα βορᾶς πέρι μητίσασθαι.

136
οὐ παύσεσθε φόνοιο δυσηχέος; οὐκ ἐσορᾶτε
ἀλλήλους δάπτοντες ἀκηδείηισι νόοιο;

137
μορφὴν δ' ἀλλάξαντα πατὴρ φίλον υἱὸν ἀείρας
σφάζει ἐπευχόμενος μέγα νήπιος· οἱ δ' ἀπορεῦνται
λισσόμενον θύοντες· ὁ δ' αὖ νήκουστος ὁμοκλέων
σφάξας ἐν μεγάροισι κακὴν ἀλεγύνατο δαῖτα.
ὣς δ' αὔτως πατέρ' υἱὸς ἑλὼν καὶ μητέρα παῖδες   5
θυμὸν ἀπορραίσαντε φίλας κατὰ σάρκας ἔδουσιν.

6

τέσσαρα γὰρ πάντων ῥιζώματα πρῶτον ἄκουε·
Ζεὺς ἀργὴς Ἥρη τε φερέσβιος ἠδ᾽ Ἀιδωνεύς
Νῆστίς θ᾽, ἣ δακρύοις τέγγει κρούνωμα βρότειον.

17

δίπλ᾽ ἐρέω· τοτὲ μὲν γὰρ ἓν ηὐξήθη μόνον εἶναι
ἐκ πλεόνων, τοτὲ δ᾽ αὖ διέφυ πλέον᾽ ἐξ ἑνὸς εἶναι.
δοιὴ δὲ θνητῶν γένεσις, δοιὴ δ᾽ ἀπόλειψις·
τὴν μὲν γὰρ πάντων σύνοδος τίκτει τ᾽ ὀλέκει τε,
ἡ δὲ πάλιν διαφυομένων θρεφθεῖσα διέπτη.   5
καὶ ταῦτ᾽ ἀλλάσσοντα διαμπερὲς οὐδαμὰ λήγει,
ἄλλοτε μὲν Φιλότητι συνερχόμεν᾽ εἰς ἓν ἅπαντα,
ἄλλοτε δ᾽ αὖ δίχ᾽ ἕκαστα φορεύμενα Νείκεος ἔχθει.
<οὕτως ἧι μὲν ἓν ἐκ πλεόνων μεμάθηκε φύεσθαι>
ἠδὲ πάλιν διαφύντος ἑνὸς πλέον᾽ ἐκτελέθουσι,   10
τῆι μὲν γίγνονταί τε καὶ οὔ σφισιν ἔμπεδος αἰών·
ἧι δὲ διαλλάσσοντα διαμπερὲς οὐδαμὰ λήγει,
ταύτηι δ᾽ αἰὲν ἔασιν ἀκίνητοι κατὰ κύκλον.
ἀλλ᾽ ἄγε μύθων κλῦθι· μάθη γάρ τοι φρένας αὔξει·
ὡς γὰρ καὶ πρὶν ἔειπα πιφαύσκων πείρατα μύθων,   15
δίπλ᾽ ἐρέω· τοτὲ μὲν γὰρ ἓν ηὐξήθη μόνον εἶναι
ἐκ πλεόνων, τοτὲ δ᾽ αὖ διέφυ πλέον᾽ ἐξ ἑνὸς εἶναι,
πῦρ καὶ ὕδωρ καὶ γαῖα καὶ ἠέρος ἄπλετον ὕψος,
Νεῖκός τ᾽ οὐλόμενον δίχα τῶν, ἀτάλαντον ἁπάντηι,
καὶ Φιλότης ἐν τοῖσιν, ἴση μῆκός τε πλάτος τε·   20
τὴν σὺ νόωι δέρκευ, μηδ᾽ ὄμμασιν ἧσο τεθηπώς·
ἥτις καὶ θνητοῖσι νομίζεται ἔμφυτος ἄρθροις,
τῆι τε φίλα φρονέουσι καὶ ἄρθμια ἔργα τελοῦσι,
Γηθοσύνην καλέοντες ἐπώνυμον ἠδ᾽ Ἀφροδίτην·
τὴν οὔ τις μετὰ τοῖσιν ἑλισσομένην δεδάηκε   25
θνητὸς ἀνήρ· σὺ δ᾽ ἄκουε λόγου στόλον οὐκ ἀπατηλόν.
ταῦτα γὰρ ἰσά τε πάντα καὶ ἥλικα γένναν ἔασι,
τιμῆς δ᾽ ἄλλης ἄλλο μέδει, πάρα δ᾽ ἦθος ἑκάστωι,
ἐν δὲ μέρει κρατέουσι περιπλομένοιο χρόνοιο.
καὶ πρὸς τοῖς οὔτ᾽ ἄρ τι ἐπιγίνεται οὐδ᾽ ἀπολήγει·   30
εἴτε γὰρ ἐφθείροντο διαμπερές, οὐκέτ᾽ ἂν ἦσαν·
τοῦτο δ᾽ ἐπαυξήσειε τὸ πᾶν τί κε; καὶ πόθεν ἐλθόν;

πῆι δέ κε κἠξαπόλοιτο, ἐπεὶ τῶνδ' οὐδὲν ἔρημον;
ἀλλ' αὐτ(ὰ) ἔστιν ταῦτα, δι' ἀλλήλων δὲ θέοντα
γίγνεται ἄλλοτε ἄλλα καὶ ἠνεκὲς αἰὲν ὁμοῖα.   35

29

οὐ γὰρ ἀπὸ νώτοιο δύο κλάδοι ἀίσσονται,
οὐ πόδες, οὐ θοὰ γοῦν(α), οὐ μήδεα γεννήεντα,
ἀλλὰ σφαῖρος ἔην καὶ <πάντοθεν> ἶσος ἑαυτῶι.

28

ἀλλ' ὅ γε πάντοθεν ἶσος <ἑοῖ> καὶ πάμπαν ἀπείρων
Σφαῖρος κυκλοτερὴς μονίηι περιηγέι γαίων.

30

αὐτὰρ ἐπεὶ μέγα Νεῖκος ἐνὶ μελέεσσιν ἐθρέφθη
ἐς τιμάς τ' ἀνόρουσε τελειομένοιο χρόνοιο,
ὅς σφιν ἀμοιβαῖος πλατέος παρ' ἐλήλαται ὅρκου ...

31

πάντα γὰρ ἑξείης πελεμίζετο γυῖα θεοῖο.

134

οὐδὲ γὰρ ἀνδρομέηι κεφαλῆι κατὰ γυῖα κέκασται,
οὐ μὲν ἀπαὶ νώτοιο δύο κλάδοι ἀίσσονται,
οὐ πόδες, οὐ θοὰ γοῦν(α), οὐ μήδεα λαχνήεντα,
ἀλλὰ φρὴν ἱερὴ καὶ ἀθέσφατος ἔπλετο μοῦνον,
φροντίσι κόσμον ἅπαντα κατἵσσουσα θοῆισιν.   5

8. Plato *Symposium* 209e5–212a7

The text is based on the *Oxford Classical Text* ed. J. Burnet (Oxford 1901).

Ταῦτα μὲν οὖν τὰ ἐρωτικὰ ἴσως, ὦ Σώκρατες, κἂν σὺ
μυηθείης· τὰ δὲ τέλεα καὶ ἐποπτικά, ὧν ἕνεκα καὶ ταῦτα   210
ἔστιν, ἐάν τις ὀρθῶς μετίη, οὐκ οἶδ' εἰ οἷός τ' ἂν εἴης.
ἐρῶ μὲν οὖν, ἔφη, ἐγὼ καὶ προθυμίας οὐδὲν ἀπολείψω·
πειρῶ δὲ ἕπεσθαι, ἂν οἷός τε ἦις. δεῖ γάρ, ἔφη, τὸν ὀρθῶς
ἰόντα ἐπὶ τοῦτο τὸ πρᾶγμα ἄρχεσθαι μὲν νέον ὄντα ἰέναι   5
ἐπὶ τὰ καλὰ σώματα, καὶ πρῶτον μέν, ἐὰν ὀρθῶς ἡγῆται
ὁ ἡγούμενος, ἑνὸς αὐτὸν σώματος ἐρᾶν καὶ ἐνταῦθα γεννᾶν

λόγους καλούς, ἔπειτα δὲ αὐτὸν κατανοῆσαι ὅτι τὸ κάλλος
τὸ ἐπὶ ὁτῳοῦν σώματι τῷ ἐπὶ ἑτέρῳ σώματι ἀδελφόν ἐστι,　　b
καὶ εἰ δεῖ διώκειν τὸ ἐπ' εἴδει καλόν, πολλὴ ἄνοια μὴ οὐχ
ἕν τε καὶ ταὐτὸν ἡγεῖσθαι τὸ ἐπὶ πᾶσιν τοῖς σώμασι κάλλος·
τοῦτο δ' ἐννοήσαντα καταστῆναι πάντων τῶν καλῶν σωμάτων
ἐραστήν, ἑνὸς δὲ τὸ σφόδρα τοῦτο χαλάσαι καταφρονή-　　5
σαντα καὶ σμικρὸν ἡγησάμενον· μετὰ δὲ ταῦτα τὸ ἐν ταῖς
ψυχαῖς κάλλος τιμιώτερον ἡγήσασθαι τοῦ ἐν τῷ σώματι,
ὥστε καὶ ἐὰν ἐπιεικὴς ὢν τὴν ψυχήν τις κἂν σμικρὸν ἄνθος
ἔχῃ, ἐξαρκεῖν αὐτῷ καὶ ἐρᾶν καὶ κήδεσθαι καὶ τίκτειν λόγους　　c
τοιούτους καὶ ζητεῖν, οἵτινες ποιήσουσι βελτίους τοὺς
νέους, ἵνα ἀναγκασθῇ αὖ θεάσασθαι τὸ ἐν τοῖς ἐπιτηδεύμασι
καὶ τοῖς νόμοις καλὸν καὶ τοῦτ' ἰδεῖν ὅτι πᾶν αὐτὸ αὑτῷ
συγγενές ἐστιν, ἵνα τὸ περὶ τὸ σῶμα καλὸν σμικρόν τι　　5
ἡγήσηται εἶναι· μετὰ δὲ τὰ ἐπιτηδεύματα ἐπὶ τὰς ἐπιστήμας
ἀγαγεῖν, ἵνα ἴδῃ αὖ ἐπιστημῶν κάλλος, καὶ βλέπων πρὸς
πολὺ ἤδη τὸ καλὸν μηκέτι τὸ παρ' ἑνί, ὥσπερ οἰκέτης,　　d
ἀγαπῶν παιδαρίου κάλλος ἢ ἀνθρώπου τινὸς ἢ ἐπιτηδεύ-
ματος ἑνός, δουλεύων φαῦλος ᾖ καὶ σμικρολόγος, ἀλλ' ἐπὶ
τὸ πολὺ πέλαγος τετραμμένος τοῦ καλοῦ καὶ θεωρῶν πολλοὺς καὶ καλοὺς λόγους καὶ μεγαλοπρεπεῖς τίκτῃ καὶ διανοή-　　5
ματα ἐν φιλοσοφίᾳ ἀφθόνῳ, ἕως ἂν ἐνταῦθα ῥωσθεὶς καὶ
αὐξηθεὶς κατίδῃ τινὰ ἐπιστήμην μίαν τοιαύτην, ἥ ἐστι καλοῦ
τοιοῦδε. πειρῶ δέ μοι, ἔφη, τὸν νοῦν προσέχειν ὡς οἷόν　　e
τε μάλιστα. ὃς γὰρ ἂν μέχρι ἐνταῦθα πρὸς τὰ ἐρωτικὰ
παιδαγωγηθῇ, θεώμενος ἐφεξῆς τε καὶ ὀρθῶς τὰ καλά, πρὸς
τέλος ἤδη ἰὼν τῶν ἐρωτικῶν ἐξαίφνης κατόψεταί τι θαυ-
μαστὸν τὴν φύσιν καλόν, τοῦτο ἐκεῖνο, ὦ Σώκρατες, οὗ δὴ　　5
ἕνεκεν καὶ οἱ ἔμπροσθεν πάντες πόνοι ἦσαν, πρῶτον μὲν
ἀεὶ ὂν καὶ οὔτε γιγνόμενον οὔτε ἀπολλύμενον, οὔτε αὐξανό-　　211
μενον οὔτε φθίνον, ἔπειτα οὐ τῇ μὲν καλόν, τῇ δ' αἰσχρόν,
οὐδὲ τοτὲ μέν, τοτὲ δὲ οὔ, οὐδὲ πρὸς μὲν τὸ καλόν, πρὸς
δὲ τὸ αἰσχρόν, οὐδ' ἔνθα μὲν καλόν, ἔνθα δὲ αἰσχρόν, ὡς
τισὶ μὲν ὂν καλόν, τισὶ δὲ αἰσχρόν· οὐδ' αὖ φαντασθήσεται　　5
αὐτῷ τὸ καλὸν οἷον πρόσωπόν τι οὐδὲ χεῖρες οὐδὲ ἄλλο
οὐδὲν ὧν σῶμα μετέχει, οὐδέ τις λόγος οὐδέ τις ἐπιστήμη,
οὐδέ που ὂν ἐν ἑτέρῳ τινι, οἷον ἐν ζῴῳ ἢ ἐν γῇ ἢ ἐν οὐρανῷ
ἢ ἔν τῳ ἄλλῳ, ἀλλ' αὐτὸ καθ' αὑτὸ μεθ' αὑτοῦ μονοειδὲς ἀεὶ　　b

ὄν, τὰ δὲ ἄλλα πάντα καλὰ ἐκείνου μετέχοντα τρόπον τινὰ
τοιοῦτον, οἷον γιγνομένων τε τῶν ἄλλων καὶ ἀπολλυμένων
μηδὲν ἐκεῖνο μήτε τι πλέον μήτε ἔλαττον γίγνεσθαι μηδὲ
πάσχειν μηδέν. ὅταν δή τις ἀπὸ τῶνδε διὰ τὸ ὀρθῶς παι-   5
δεραστεῖν ἐπανιὼν ἐκεῖνο τὸ καλὸν ἄρχηται καθορᾶν, σχεδὸν
ἄν τι ἅπτοιτο τοῦ τέλους. τοῦτο γὰρ δή ἐστι τὸ ὀρθῶς ἐπὶ
τὰ ἐρωτικὰ ἰέναι ἢ ὑπ᾽ ἄλλου ἄγεσθαι, ἀρχόμενον ἀπὸ   c
τῶνδε τῶν καλῶν ἐκείνου ἕνεκα τοῦ καλοῦ ἀεὶ ἐπανιέναι,
ὥσπερ ἐπαναβασμοῖς χρώμενον, ἀπὸ ἑνὸς ἐπὶ δύο καὶ ἀπὸ
δυοῖν ἐπὶ πάντα τὰ καλὰ σώματα, καὶ ἀπὸ τῶν καλῶν
σωμάτων ἐπὶ τὰ καλὰ ἐπιτηδεύματα, καὶ ἀπὸ τῶν ἐπιτηδευ-   5
μάτων ἐπὶ τὰ καλὰ μαθήματα, καὶ ἀπὸ τῶν μαθημάτων ἐπ᾽
ἐκεῖνο τὸ μάθημα τελευτῆσαι, ὅ ἐστιν οὐκ ἄλλου ἢ αὐτοῦ
ἐκείνου τοῦ καλοῦ μάθημα, [ἵνα] καὶ γνῷ αὐτὸ τελευτῶν ὃ ἔστι
καλόν. ἐνταῦθα τοῦ βίου, ὦ φίλε Σώκρατες, ἔφη ἡ Μαν-   d
τινικὴ ξένη, εἴπερ που ἄλλοθι, βιωτὸν ἀνθρώπῳ, θεωμένῳ
αὐτὸ τὸ καλόν. ὃ ἐάν ποτε ἴδῃς, οὐ κατὰ χρυσίον τε καὶ
ἐσθῆτα καὶ τοὺς καλοὺς παῖδάς τε καὶ νεανίσκους δόξει σοι
εἶναι, οὓς νῦν ὁρῶν ἐκπέπληξαι καὶ ἕτοιμος εἶ καὶ σὺ καὶ   5
ἄλλοι πολλοί, ὁρῶντες τὰ παιδικὰ καὶ συνόντες ἀεὶ αὐτοῖς,
εἴ πως οἷόν τ᾽ ἦν, μήτ᾽ ἐσθίειν μήτε πίνειν, ἀλλὰ θεᾶσθαι
μόνον καὶ συνεῖναι. τί δῆτα, ἔφη, οἰόμεθα, εἴ τῳ γένοιτο
αὐτὸ τὸ καλὸν ἰδεῖν εἰλικρινές, καθαρόν, ἄμεικτον, ἀλλὰ   e
μὴ ἀνάπλεων σαρκῶν τε ἀνθρωπίνων καὶ χρωμάτων καὶ
ἄλλης πολλῆς φλυαρίας θνητῆς, ἀλλ᾽ αὐτὸ τὸ θεῖον καλὸν
δύναιτο μονοειδὲς κατιδεῖν; ἆρ᾽ οἴει, ἔφη, φαῦλον βίον
γίγνεσθαι ἐκεῖσε βλέποντος ἀνθρώπου καὶ ἐκεῖνο ᾧ δεῖ   **212**
θεωμένου καὶ συνόντος αὐτῷ; ἢ οὐκ ἐνθυμῇ, ἔφη, ὅτι ἐνταῦθα
αὐτῷ μοναχοῦ γενήσεται, ὁρῶντι ᾧ ὁρατὸν τὸ καλόν, τίκτειν
οὐκ εἴδωλα ἀρετῆς, ἅτε οὐκ εἰδώλου ἐφαπτομένῳ, ἀλλὰ
ἀληθῆ, ἅτε τοῦ ἀληθοῦς ἐφαπτομένῳ· τεκόντι δὲ ἀρετὴν   5
ἀληθῆ καὶ θρεψαμένῳ ὑπάρχει θεοφιλεῖ γενέσθαι, καὶ εἴπέρ
τῳ ἄλλῳ ἀνθρώπων ἀθανάτῳ καὶ ἐκείνῳ;

9. Aristotle *Nicomachean Ethics* 1177b26–1179a23

The text is based on the *Oxford Classical Text* ed. I. Bywater (Oxford 1894).

ὁ δὲ τοιοῦτος ἂν εἴη βίος κρείττων ἢ
κατ᾽ ἄνθρωπον· οὐ γὰρ ᾗ ἄνθρωπός ἐστιν οὕτω βιώσεται, ἀλλ᾽
ᾗ θεῖόν τι ἐν αὐτῷ ὑπάρχει· ὅσον δὲ διαφέρει τοῦτο τοῦ συνθέτου, τοσοῦτον καὶ ἡ ἐνέργεια τῆς κατὰ τὴν ἄλλην ἀρετήν.
εἰ δὴ θεῖον ὁ νοῦς πρὸς τὸν ἄνθρωπον, καὶ ὁ κατὰ τοῦτον βίος
θεῖος πρὸς τὸν ἀνθρώπινον βίον. οὐ χρὴ δὲ κατὰ τοὺς παραι-
νοῦντας ἀνθρώπινα φρονεῖν ἄνθρωπον ὄντα οὐδὲ θνητὰ τὸν
θνητόν, ἀλλ᾽ ἐφ᾽ ὅσον ἐνδέχεται ἀθανατίζειν καὶ πάντα ποιεῖν
πρὸς τὸ ζῆν κατὰ τὸ κράτιστον τῶν ἐν αὐτῷ· εἰ γὰρ καὶ
τῷ ὄγκῳ μικρόν ἐστι, δυνάμει καὶ τιμιότητι πολὺ μᾶλλον   1178a
πάντων ὑπερέχει. δόξειε δ᾽ ἂν καὶ εἶναι ἕκαστος τοῦτο, εἴπερ
τὸ κύριον καὶ ἄμεινον. ἄτοπον οὖν γίνοιτ᾽ ἄν, εἰ μὴ τὸν
αὑτοῦ βίον αἱροῖτο ἀλλά τινος ἄλλου. τὸ λεχθέν τε πρότερον ἁρμόσει καὶ νῦν· τὸ γὰρ οἰκεῖον ἑκάστῳ τῇ φύσει κράτιστον καὶ ἥδιστόν ἐστιν ἑκάστῳ· καὶ τῷ ἀνθρώπῳ δὴ ὁ κατὰ
τὸν νοῦν βίος, εἴπερ τοῦτο μάλιστα ἄνθρωπος. οὗτος ἄρα καὶ
εὐδαιμονέστατος.

Δευτέρως δ᾽ ὁ κατὰ τὴν ἄλλην ἀρετήν· αἱ γὰρ κατὰ
ταύτην ἐνέργειαι ἀνθρωπικαί. δίκαια γὰρ καὶ ἀνδρεῖα καὶ τὰ
ἄλλα τὰ κατὰ τὰς ἀρετὰς πρὸς ἀλλήλους πράττομεν ἐν
συναλλάγμασι καὶ χρείαις καὶ πράξεσι παντοίαις ἔν τε
τοῖς πάθεσι διατηροῦντες τὸ πρέπον ἑκάστῳ· ταῦτα δ᾽ εἶναι
φαίνεται πάντα ἀνθρωπικά. ἔνια δὲ καὶ συμβαίνειν ἀπὸ
τοῦ σώματος δοκεῖ, καὶ πολλὰ συνῳκειῶσθαι τοῖς πάθεσιν
ἡ τοῦ ἤθους ἀρετή. συνέζευκται δὲ καὶ ἡ φρόνησις τῇ τοῦ
ἤθους ἀρετῇ, καὶ αὕτη τῇ φρονήσει, εἴπερ αἱ μὲν τῆς φρο-
νήσεως ἀρχαὶ κατὰ τὰς ἠθικάς εἰσιν ἀρετάς, τὸ δ᾽ ὀρθὸν
τῶν ἠθικῶν κατὰ τὴν φρόνησιν. συνηρτημέναι δ᾽ αὗται καὶ
τοῖς πάθεσι περὶ τὸ σύνθετον ἂν εἶεν· αἱ δὲ τοῦ συνθέτου ἀρε-
ταὶ ἀνθρωπικαί· καὶ ὁ βίος δὴ ὁ κατὰ ταύτας καὶ ἡ εὐδαιμονία. ἡ δὲ τοῦ νοῦ κεχωρισμένη· τοσοῦτον γὰρ περὶ αὐτῆς
εἰρήσθω· διακριβῶσαι γὰρ μεῖζον τοῦ προκειμένου ἐστίν. δόξειε
δ᾽ ἂν καὶ τῆς ἐκτὸς χορηγίας ἐπὶ μικρὸν ἢ ἐπ᾽ ἔλαττον δεῖ-
σθαι τῆς ἠθικῆς. τῶν μὲν γὰρ ἀναγκαίων ἀμφοῖν χρεία
καὶ ἐξ ἴσου ἔστω, εἰ καὶ μᾶλλον διαπονεῖ περὶ τὸ σῶμα ὁ

πολιτικός, καὶ ὅσα τοιαῦτα· μικρὸν γὰρ ἄν τι διαφέροι·
πρὸς δὲ τὰς ἐνεργείας πολὺ διοίσει. τῷ μὲν γὰρ ἐλευθερίῳ
δεήσει χρημάτων πρὸς τὸ πράττειν τὰ ἐλευθέρια, καὶ τῷ
δικαίῳ δὴ εἰς τὰς ἀνταποδόσεις (αἱ γὰρ βουλήσεις ἄδηλοι,
προσποιοῦνται δὲ καὶ οἱ μὴ δίκαιοι βούλεσθαι δικαιοπραγεῖν),
τῷ ἀνδρείῳ δὲ δυνάμεως, εἴπερ ἐπιτελεῖ τι τῶν κατὰ τὴν
ἀρετήν, καὶ τῷ σώφρονι ἐξουσίας· πῶς γὰρ δῆλος ἔσται ἢ
οὗτος ἢ τῶν ἄλλων τις; ἀμφισβητεῖταί τε πότερον κυριώτε-
ρον τῆς ἀρετῆς ἡ προαίρεσις ἢ αἱ πράξεις, ὡς ἐν ἀμφοῖν
οὔσης· τὸ δὴ τέλειον δῆλον ὡς ἐν ἀμφοῖν ἂν εἴη· πρὸς δὲ   1178b
τὰς πράξεις πολλῶν δεῖται, καὶ ὅσῳ ἂν μείζους ὦσι καὶ
καλλίους, πλειόνων. τῷ δὲ θεωροῦντι οὐδενὸς τῶν τοιούτων
πρός γε τὴν ἐνέργειαν χρεία, ἀλλ᾽ ὡς εἰπεῖν καὶ ἐμπόδιά ἐστι
πρός γε τὴν θεωρίαν· ᾗ δ᾽ ἄνθρωπός ἐστι καὶ πλείοσι συζῇ,
αἱρεῖται τὰ κατὰ τὴν ἀρετὴν πράττειν· δεήσεται οὖν τῶν τοιούτων πρὸς τὸ ἀνθρωπεύεσθαι. ἡ δὲ τελεία εὐδαιμονία ὅτι θεωρη-
τική τις ἐστιν ἐνέργεια, καὶ ἐντεῦθεν ἂν φανείη. τοὺς θεοὺς
γὰρ μάλιστα ὑπειλήφαμεν μακαρίους καὶ εὐδαίμονας εἶναι·
πράξεις δὲ ποίας ἀπονεῖμαι χρεὼν αὐτοῖς; πότερα τὰς δι-
καίας; ἢ γελοῖοι φανοῦνται συναλλάττοντες καὶ παρακατα-
θήκας ἀποδιδόντες καὶ ὅσα τοιαῦτα; ἀλλὰ τὰς ἀνδρείους
ὑπομένοντας τὰ φοβερὰ καὶ κινδυνεύοντας ὅτι καλόν; ἢ
τὰς ἐλευθερίους; τίνι δὲ δώσουσιν; ἄτοπον δ᾽ εἰ καὶ ἔσται
αὐτοῖς νόμισμα ἤ τι τοιοῦτον. αἱ δὲ σώφρονες τί ἂν εἶεν;
ἢ φορτικὸς ὁ ἔπαινος, ὅτι οὐκ ἔχουσι φαύλας ἐπιθυμίας;
διεξιοῦσι δὲ πάντα φαίνοιτ᾽ ἂν τὰ περὶ τὰς πράξεις μικρὰ
καὶ ἀνάξια θεῶν. ἀλλὰ μὴν ζῆν γε πάντες ὑπειλήφασιν
αὐτοὺς καὶ ἐνεργεῖν ἄρα· οὐ γὰρ δὴ καθεύδειν ὥσπερ τὸν
Ἐνδυμίωνα. τῷ δὴ ζῶντι τοῦ πράττειν ἀφαιρουμένου, ἔτι δὲ
μᾶλλον τοῦ ποιεῖν, τί λείπεται πλὴν θεωρία; ὥστε ἡ τοῦ θεοῦ
ἐνέργεια, μακαριότητι διαφέρουσα, θεωρητικὴ ἂν εἴη· καὶ
τῶν ἀνθρωπίνων δὴ ἡ ταύτῃ συγγενεστάτη εὐδαιμονικωτάτη.
σημεῖον δὲ καὶ τὸ μὴ μετέχειν τὰ λοιπὰ ζῷα εὐδαιμονίας,
τῆς τοιαύτης ἐνεργείας ἐστερημένα τελείως. τοῖς μὲν γὰρ
θεοῖς ἅπας ὁ βίος μακάριος, τοῖς δ᾽ ἀνθρώποις, ἐφ᾽ ὅσον
ὁμοίωμά τι τῆς τοιαύτης ἐνεργείας ὑπάρχει· τῶν δ᾽ ἄλλων
ζῴων οὐδὲν εὐδαιμονεῖ, ἐπειδὴ οὐδαμῇ κοινωνεῖ θεωρίας. ἐφ᾽
ὅσον δὴ διατείνει ἡ θεωρία, καὶ ἡ εὐδαιμονία, καὶ οἷς μᾶλ-

λον ὑπάρχει τὸ θεωρεῖν, καὶ εὐδαιμονεῖν, οὐ κατὰ συμβε-
βηκὸς ἀλλὰ κατὰ τὴν θεωρίαν· αὕτη γὰρ καθ' αὑτὴν τιμία.
ὥστ' εἴη ἂν ἡ εὐδαιμονία θεωρία τις.

Δεήσει δὲ καὶ τῆς ἐκτὸς εὐημερίας ἀνθρώπῳ ὄντι· οὐ γὰρ
αὐτάρκης ἡ φύσις πρὸς τὸ θεωρεῖν, ἀλλὰ δεῖ καὶ τὸ σῶμα
ὑγιαίνειν καὶ τροφὴν καὶ τὴν λοιπὴν θεραπείαν ὑπάρχειν.
οὐ μὴν οἰητέον γε πολλῶν καὶ μεγάλων δεήσεσθαι τὸν εὐδαι-   1179a
μονήσοντα, εἰ μὴ ἐνδέχεται ἄνευ τῶν ἐκτὸς ἀγαθῶν μα-
κάριον εἶναι· οὐ γὰρ ἐν τῇ ὑπερβολῇ τὸ αὔταρκες οὐδ' ἡ πρᾶ-
ξις, δυνατὸν δὲ καὶ μὴ ἄρχοντα γῆς καὶ θαλάττης πράττειν τὰ καλά· καὶ γὰρ ἀπὸ μετρίων δύναιτ' ἄν τις πράττειν
κατὰ τὴν ἀρετήν (τοῦτο δ' ἔστιν ἰδεῖν ἐναργῶς· οἱ γὰρ ἰδιῶ-
ται τῶν δυναστῶν οὐχ ἧττον δοκοῦσι τὰ ἐπιεικῆ πράττειν,
ἀλλὰ καὶ μᾶλλον)· ἱκανὸν δὲ τοσαῦθ' ὑπάρχειν· ἔσται γὰρ ὁ
βίος εὐδαίμων τοῦ κατὰ τὴν ἀρετὴν ἐνεργοῦντος. καὶ Σόλων
δὲ τοὺς εὐδαίμονας ἴσως ἀπεφαίνετο καλῶς, εἰπὼν μετρίως
τοῖς ἐκτὸς κεχορηγημένους, πεπραγότας δὲ τὰ κάλλισθ', ὡς
ᾤετο, καὶ βεβιωκότας σωφρόνως· ἐνδέχεται γὰρ μέτρια
κεκτημένους πράττειν ἃ δεῖ. ἔοικε δὲ καὶ Ἀναξαγόρας οὐ
πλούσιον οὐδὲ δυνάστην ὑπολαβεῖν τὸν εὐδαίμονα, εἰπὼν ὅτι
οὐκ ἂν θαυμάσειεν εἴ τις ἄτοπος φανείη τοῖς πολλοῖς· οὗτοι
γὰρ κρίνουσι τοῖς ἐκτός, τούτων αἰσθανόμενοι μόνον. συμφω-
νεῖν δὴ τοῖς λόγοις ἐοίκασιν αἱ τῶν σοφῶν δόξαι. πίστιν
μὲν οὖν καὶ τὰ τοιαῦτα ἔχει τινά, τὸ δ' ἀληθὲς ἐν τοῖς
πρακτικοῖς ἐκ τῶν ἔργων καὶ τοῦ βίου κρίνεται· ἐν τούτοις
γὰρ τὸ κύριον. σκοπεῖν δὴ τὰ προειρημένα χρὴ ἐπὶ τὰ ἔργα
καὶ τὸν βίον φέροντας, καὶ συναδόντων μὲν τοῖς ἔργοις
ἀποδεκτέον, διαφωνούντων δὲ λόγους ὑποληπτέον. ὁ δὲ κατὰ
νοῦν ἐνεργῶν καὶ τοῦτον θεραπεύων καὶ διακείμενος ἄριστα καὶ
θεοφιλέστατος ἔοικεν.

10. Hippocratic 'On the Sacred Disease' 1–6

The text is based on the edition by W. H. S. Jones in the Loeb series (London and New York 1923).

ΠΕΡΙ ΙΕΡΗΣ ΝΟΣΟΥ

1. Περὶ τῆς ἱερῆς νούσου καλεομένης ὧδ' ἔχει· οὐδέν τί μοι δοκεῖ
τῶν ἄλλων θειοτέρη εἶναι νούσων οὐδὲ ἱερωτέρη, ἀλλὰ φύσιν μὲν
ἔχει καὶ πρόφασιν, οἱ δ' ἄνθρωποι ἐνόμισαν θεῖόν τι πρῆγμα εἶναι ὑπὸ ἀπει-
ρίης καὶ θαυμασιότητος, ὅτι οὐδὲν ἔοικεν ἑτέρῃσι νούσοισιν· καὶ κατὰ
μὲν τὴν ἀπορίην αὐτοῖσι τοῦ μὴ γινώσκειν τὸ θεῖον διασώζε-   5
ται, κατὰ δὲ τὴν εὐπορίην τοῦ τρόπου τῆς ἰήσιος ᾧ ἰῶνται, ἀπόλλυται, ὅτι καθαρμοῖσί τε ἰῶνται καὶ ἐπαοιδῇσιν. εἰ δὲ διὰ τὸ θαυ-
μάσιον θεῖον νομιεῖται, πολλὰ τὰ ἱερὰ νουσήματα ἔσται καὶ οὐχὶ ἕν,
ὡς ἐγὼ ἀποδείξω ἕτερα οὐδὲν ἧσσον ἐόντα θαυμάσια οὐδὲ τερατώδεα,
ἃ οὐδεὶς νομίζει ἱερὰ εἶναι. τοῦτο μὲν οἱ πυρετοὶ οἱ ἀμφημερι-   10
νοὶ καὶ οἱ τριταῖοι καὶ οἱ τεταρταῖοι οὐδὲν ἧσσόν μοι δοκέουσιν
ἱεροὶ εἶναι καὶ ὑπὸ θεοῦ γίνεσθαι ταύτης τῆς νούσου, ὧν οὐ θαυμα-
σίως ἔχουσιν· τοῦτο δὲ ὁρῶ μαινομένους ἀνθρώπους καὶ παραφρονέοντας ἀπὸ οὐδεμιῆς προφάσιος ἐμφανέος, καὶ πολλά τε καὶ
ἄκαιρα ποιέοντας, ἔν τε τῷ ὕπνῳ οἶδα πολλοὺς οἰμώζοντας καὶ βοῶν-   15
τας, τοὺς δὲ πνιγομένους, τοὺς δὲ καὶ ἀναΐσσοντάς τε καὶ φεύγον-
τας ἔξω καὶ παραφρονέοντας μέχρι ἐπέγρωνται, ἔπειτα δὲ ὑγιέας
ἐόντας καὶ φρονέοντας ὥσπερ καὶ πρότερον, ἐόντας τ' αὐτοὺς
ὠχρούς τε καὶ ἀσθενέας, καὶ ταῦτα οὐχ ἅπαξ, ἀλλὰ πολλάκις. ἄλλα
τε πολλά ἐστι καὶ παντοδαπὰ ὧν περὶ ἑκάστου λέγειν πουλὺς ἂν εἴη   20
λόγος.

2. ἐμοὶ δὲ δοκέουσιν οἱ πρῶτοι τοῦτο τὸ νόσημα ἱερώσαντες
τοιοῦτοι εἶναι ἄνθρωποι οἷοι καὶ νῦν εἰσι μάγοι τε καὶ καθάρται καὶ
ἀγύρται καὶ ἀλαζόνες, οὗτοι δὲ καὶ προσποιέονται σφόδρα θεοσεβέες
εἶναι καὶ πλέον τι εἰδέναι. οὗτοι τοίνυν παραμπεχόμενοι καὶ προ-
βαλλόμενοι τὸ θεῖον τῆς ἀμηχανίης τοῦ μὴ ἔχειν ὅ τι προσενέγ-   5
καντες ὠφελήσουσιν, καὶ ὡς μὴ κατάδηλοι ἔωσιν οὐδὲν ἐπιστάμενοι,
ἱερὸν ἐνόμισαν τοῦτο τὸ πάθος εἶναι· καὶ λόγους ἐπιλέξαντες ἐπιτη-
δείους τὴν ἴησιν κατεστήσαντο ἐς τὸ ἀσφαλὲς σφίσιν αὐτοῖσι, καθαρ-
μοὺς προσφέροντες καὶ ἐπαοιδὰς, λουτρῶν τε ἀπέχεσθαι κελεύοντες
καὶ ἐδεσμάτων πολλῶν καὶ ἀνεπιτηδείων ἀνθρώποισι νοσέουσιν   10
ἐσθίειν, θαλασσίων μὲν τρίγλης, μελανούρου, κεστρέος, ἐγχέλυος

(οὗτοι γὰρ οἱ ἰχθύες ἐπικηρότατοί εἰσιν), κρεῶν δὲ αἰγείων καὶ ἐλά-
φων καὶ χοιρίων καὶ κυνὸς (ταῦτα γὰρ κρεῶν ταρακτικώτατά ἐστι
τῆς κοιλίης), ὀρνίθων δὲ ἀλεκτρυόνος καὶ τρυγόνος καὶ ὠτίδος, ἔτι
δὲ ὅσα νομίζεται ἰσχυρότατα εἶναι, λαχάνων δὲ μίνθης,	15
σκορόδου καὶ κρομμύων (δριμὺ γὰρ ἀσθενέοντι οὐδὲν ξυμφέρει),
ἱμάτιον δὲ μέλαν μὴ ἔχειν (θανατῶδες γὰρ τὸ μέλαν), μηδὲ ἐν αἰγείῳ
κατακέεσθαι δέρματι μηδὲ φορέειν, μηδὲ πόδα ἐπὶ ποδὶ ἔχειν, μηδὲ
χεῖρα ἐπὶ χειρὶ (πάντα γὰρ ταῦτα κωλύματα εἶναι). ταῦτα δὲ τοῦ θείου
εἴνεκα προστιθέασιν, ὡς πλέον τι εἰδότες καὶ ἄλλας προφάσιας λέ-	20
γοντες, ὅπως, εἰ μὲν ὑγιὴς γένοιτο, αὐτῶν ἡ δόξα εἴη καὶ ἡ δεξιό-
της, εἰ δὲ ἀποθάνοι, ἐν ἀσφαλεῖ καθισταῖντο αὐτῶν αἱ ἀπολογίαι καὶ
ἔχοιεν πρόφασιν ὡς οὐδὲν αἴτιοί εἰσιν, ἀλλ᾽ οἱ θεοί· οὔτε γὰρ
φαγεῖν οὔτε πιεῖν ἔδοσαν φάρμακον οὐδέν, οὔτε λουτροῖσι καθήψη-
σαν, ὥστε δοκεῖν αἴτιοι εἶναι. ἐγὼ δὲ δοκῶ Λιβύων τῶν τὴν με-	25
σόγειον οἰκεόντων οὐδέν᾽ ἂν ὑγιαίνειν, ὅτι ἐν αἰγείοισι δέρμασι κατα-
κέονται καὶ κρέασιν αἰγείοισι χρέονται, ἐπεὶ οὐκ ἔχουσιν οὔτε στρῶμα
οὔτε ἱμάτιον οὔτε ὑπόδημα ὅ τι μὴ αἴγειόν ἐστιν· οὐ γάρ ἐστιν αὐτοῖς ἄλλο προβάτιον οὐδὲν ἢ αἶγες καὶ βόες. εἰ δὲ ταῦτα ἐσθιόμενα
καὶ προσφερόμενα τὴν νοῦσον τίκτει τε καὶ αὔξει καὶ μὴ ἐσθιόμενα	30
ἰῆται, οὐκέτι ὁ θεὸς αἴτιος ἐστίν, οὐδὲ οἱ καθαρμοὶ ὠφελέουσιν,
ἀλλὰ τὰ ἐδέσματα τὰ ἰώμενά ἐστι καὶ τὰ βλάπτοντα, τοῦ δὲ θεοῦ
ἀφανίζεται ἡ δύναμις.

3. οὕτως οὖν ἔμοιγε δοκέουσιν οἵτινες τούτῳ τῷ τρόπῳ
ἐγχειρέουσιν ἰῆσθαι ταῦτα τὰ νοσήματα, οὔτε ἱερὰ
νομίζειν εἶναι οὔτε θεῖα· ὅπου γὰρ ὑπὸ καθαρμῶν τοιούτων μετά-
στατα γίνεται καὶ ὑπὸ θεραπείης τοιῆσδε, τί κωλύει καὶ ὑφ᾽ ἑτέρων
τεχνημάτων ὁμοίων τούτοισιν ἐπιγίνεσθαι τοῖσιν ἀνθρώποισι καὶ	5
προσπίπτειν; ὥστε τὸ θεῖον μηκέτι αἴτιον εἶναι, ἀλλά τι ἀνθρώπινον.
ὅστις γὰρ οἷός τε περικαθαίρων ἐστὶ καὶ μαγεύων ἀπάγειν τοιοῦτον πάθος, οὗτος κἂν ἐπάγοι ἕτερα τεχνησάμενος, καὶ ἐν τούτῳ τῷ
λόγῳ τὸ θεῖον ἀπόλλυται. τοιαῦτα λέγοντες καὶ μηχανώμενοι προσ-
ποιέονται πλέον τι εἰδέναι, καὶ ἀνθρώπους ἐξαπατῶσι προστιθέμενοι	10
αὐτοῖς ἁγνείας τε καὶ καθάρσιας, ὅ τε πολὺς αὐτοῖς τοῦ λόγου ἐς τὸ θεῖον ἀφήκει καὶ τὸ δαιμόνιον. καίτοι ἔμοιγε οὐ περὶ εὐ-
σεβείης δοκέουσι τοὺς λόγους ποιεῖσθαι, ὡς οἴονται, ἀλλὰ περὶ ἀ-
σεβείης μᾶλλον, καὶ ὡς οἱ θεοὶ οὐκ εἰσὶ, τό τε εὐσεβὲς αὐτῶν
καὶ τὸ θεῖον ἀσεβές ἐστιν καὶ ἀνόσιον, ὡς ἐγὼ διδάξω.	15

4.   εἰ γὰρ σελήνην καθαιρεῖν καὶ ἥλιον
ἀφανίζειν καὶ χειμῶνά τε καὶ εὐδίην ποιεῖν καὶ ὄμβρους καὶ
αὐχμοὺς καὶ θάλασσαν ἄπορον καὶ γῆν ἄφορον καὶ τἄλλα
τὰ τοιουτότροπα πάντα ὑποδέχονται ἐπίστασθαι, εἴτε καὶ ἐκ τελε-
τέων εἴτε καὶ ἐξ ἄλλης τινὸς γνώμης ἢ μελέτης φασὶν ταῦτα οἷόν   5
τ' εἶναι γενέσθαι οἱ ταῦτ' ἐπιτηδεύοντες, δυσσεβεῖν ἔμοιγε δοκέουσι
καὶ θεοὺς οὔτε εἶναι νομίζειν οὔτε ἰσχύειν οὐδὲν οὔτε εἴργε-
σθαι ἂν οὐδενὸς τῶν ἐσχάτων, ἃ ποιέοντες πῶς οὐ δεινοὶ αὐτοῖς
εἰσίν; εἰ γὰρ ἄνθρωπος μαγεύων καὶ θύων σελήνην τε καθαιρή-
σει καὶ ἥλιον ἀφανιεῖ καὶ χειμῶνα καὶ εὐδίην ποιήσει, οὐκ ἂν ἔγωγέ   10
τι θεῖον νομίσαιμι τούτων εἶναι οὐδέν, ἀλλ' ἀνθρώπινον, εἰ δὴ τοῦ θείου ἡ
δύναμις ὑπὸ ἀνθρώπου γνώμης κρατεῖται καὶ δεδούλωται. ἴσως δὲ
οὐχ οὕτως ἔχει ταῦτα, ἀλλ' ἄνθρωποι βίου δεόμενοι πολλὰ καὶ παντοῖα τεχνῶνται καὶ ποικίλλουσιν ἔς τε τἄλλα πάντα καὶ ἐς τὴν νοῦσον ταύτην, ἑκάστῳ εἴδει τοῦ πάθεος θεῷ τὴν αἰτίην προστιθέντες.   15
καὶ ἢν μὲν γὰρ αἶγα μιμῶνται, καὶ ἢν βρύχωνται, ἢ τὰ δεξιὰ
σπῶνται, μητέρα θεῶν φασὶν αἰτίην εἶναι. ἢν δὲ ὀξύτερον καὶ εὐτονώτερον
φθέγγηται, ἵππῳ εἰκάζουσι, καὶ φασὶ Ποσειδῶνα αἴτιον εἶναι. ἢν δὲ καὶ τῆς
κόπρου τι παρῇ, ὅσα πολλάκις γίνεται ὑπὸ τῆς νούσου βιαζομένοισιν,
Ἐνοδίου πρόσκειται ἡ προσωνυμίη· ἢν δὲ λεπτότερον καὶ πυκνότε-   20
ρον, οἷον ὄρνιθες, Ἀπόλλων νόμιος. ἢν δὲ ἀφρὸν ἐκ τοῦ στόματος
ἀφίῃ καὶ τοῖσι ποσὶ λακτίζῃ, Ἄρης τὴν αἰτίην ἔχει. οἷσι δὲ νυκτὸς
δείματα παρίσταται καὶ φόβοι καὶ παράνοιαι καὶ ἀναπηδήσιες
ἐκ τῆς κλίνης καὶ φεύξιες ἔξω, Ἑκάτης φασὶν εἶναι ἐπιβολὰς
καὶ ἡρώων ἐφόδους. καθαρμοῖσί τε χρέονται καὶ ἐπαοιδῇσι,   25
καὶ ἀνοσιώτατόν τε καὶ ἀθεώτατον πρῆγμα ποιέουσιν, ὡς ἔμοιγε δοκεῖ·
καθαίρουσι γὰρ τοὺς ἐχομένους τῇ νούσῳ αἵματί τε καὶ ἄλλοισι
τοιούτοις ὥσπερ μίασμά τι ἔχοντας, ἢ ἀλάστορας, ἢ πεφαρμακευμέ-
νους ὑπὸ ἀνθρώπων, ἤ τι ἔργον ἀνόσιον εἰργασμένους, οὓς ἐχρῆν
τἀναντία τούτων ποιεῖν, θύειν τε καὶ εὔχεσθαι καὶ ἐς τὰ ἱερὰ φέ-   30
ροντας ἱκετεύειν τοὺς θεούς· νῦν δὲ τούτων μὲν ποιέουσιν οὐδέν, καθαίρουσι δέ. καὶ τὰ μὲν τῶν καθαρμῶν γῇ κρύπτουσι, τὰ δὲ ἐς θάλασσαν ἐμβάλλουσι, τὰ δὲ ἐς τὰ ὄρεα ἀποφέρουσιν, ὅπῃ μηδεὶς
ἅψεται μηδὲ ἐπιβήσεται· τὰ δ' ἐχρῆν ἐς τὰ ἱερὰ φέροντας τῷ θεῷ
ἀποδοῦναι, εἰ δὴ ὁ θεός ἐστιν αἴτιος. οὐ μέντοι ἔγωγε ἀξιῶ ὑπὸ θεοῦ   35
ἀνθρώπου σῶμα μιαίνεσθαι, τὸ ἐπικηρότατον ὑπὸ τοῦ ἁγνοτάτου·
ἀλλὰ καὶ ἢν τυγχάνῃ ὑπὸ ἑτέρου μεμιασμένον ἤ τι πεπονθός, ὑπὸ τοῦ
θεοῦ καθαίρεσθαι ἂν αὐτὸ καὶ ἁγνίζεσθαι μᾶλλον ἢ μιαίνεσθαι. τὰ

γοῦν μέγιστα τῶν ἁμαρτημάτων καὶ ἀνοσιώτατα τὸ θεῖόν ἐστι τὸ
καθαῖρον καὶ ἁγνίζον καὶ ῥύμμα γινόμενον ἡμῖν, αὐτοί τε ὅρους   40
τοῖσι θεοῖσι τῶν ἱερῶν καὶ τῶν τεμενέων ἀποδείκνυμεν, ὡς ἂν μηδεὶς ὑπερβαίνῃ ἢν μὴ ἁγνεύῃ, εἰσιόντες τε ἡμεῖς περιρραινόμεθα οὐχ
ὡς μιαινόμενοι, ἀλλ' εἴ τι καὶ πρότερον ἔχομεν μύσος, τοῦτο ἀφαγνιού-
μενοι. καὶ περὶ μὲν τῶν καθαρμῶν οὕτω μοι δοκεῖ ἔχειν.

5.   τὸ δὲ νόσημα τοῦτο οὐδέν τί μοι δοκεῖ θειότερον
εἶναι τῶν λοιπῶν, ἀλλὰ φύσιν ἔχει ἣν καὶ τὰ ἄλλα νοσήματα,
καὶ πρόφασιν ὅθεν ἕκαστα γίνεται· καὶ ἰητὸν εἶναι, καὶ
οὐδὲν ἧσσον ἑτέρων, ὅ τι ἂν μὴ ἤδη ὑπὸ χρόνου πολλοῦ καταβεβια-
σμένον ᾖ, ὥστε ἤδη ἰσχυρότερον εἶναι τῶν φαρμάκων τῶν προσφε-   5
ρομένων. ἄρχεται δὲ ὥσπερ καὶ τἄλλα νοσήματα κατὰ γένος· εἰ
γὰρ ἐκ φλεγματώδεος φλεγματώδης, καὶ ἐκ χολώδεος χολώδης γίνεται, καὶ ἐκ φθινώδεος φθινώδης, καὶ ἐκ σπληνώδεος σπληνώδης, τί
κωλύει ὅτῳ πατὴρ καὶ μήτηρ εἴχετο νοσήματι, τούτῳ καὶ τῶν
ἐκγόνων ἔχεσθαί τινα; ὡς ὁ γόνος ἔρχεται πάντοθεν τοῦ σώματος,   10
ἀπό τε τῶν ὑγιηρῶν ὑγιηρός, καὶ ἀπὸ τῶν νοσερῶν νοσερός. ἕτερον
δὲ μέγα τεκμήριον ὅτι οὐδὲν θειότερόν ἐστι τῶν λοιπῶν νοσημά-
των· τοῖσι γὰρ φλεγματώδεσι φύσει γίνεται· τοῖσι δὲ χολώδεσιν οὐ
προσπίπτει· καίτοι εἰ θειότερόν ἐστι τῶν ἄλλων, τοῖσιν ἅπασιν
ὁμοίως ἔδει γίνεσθαι τὴν νοῦσον ταύτην, καὶ μὴ διακρίνειν μήτε χο-   15
λώδεα μήτε φλεγματώδεα.

6. ἀλλὰ γὰρ αἴτιος ὁ ἐγκέφαλος τούτου τοῦ πάθεος, ὥσπερ καὶ
τῶν ἄλλων νοσημάτων τῶν μεγίστων· ὅτῳ δὲ τρόπῳ καὶ ἐξ οἵης
προφάσιος γίνεται, ἐγὼ φράσω σαφέως.

11. *Lex Sacra* from Selinous: Pollution

The text is based on that in *A Lex Sacra from Selinous*, by Michael H. Jameson,
David R. Jordan, Roy D. Kotansky, Greek, Roman, and Byzantine Monographs
11 (Duke University, Durham, North Carolina 1993). Continuous capital letters
indicate letters that cannot be divided into identifiable words.

Column A

3 καταλ[ε]ίποντας, κατ*h*αιγίζεν δὲ τὸς *h*ομοσεπύος
7 τὸν *h*ιαρὸν *h*α θυσία πρὸ Ϙοτυτίον καὶ τὰς ἐχεχερίας πένπ[τοι]
8 Ϝέτει *h*ôιπερ *h*όκα *h*α Ὀλυνπιὰς ποτεί̈ε. τôι Διὶ τôι Εὐμενεῖ θύ[ε]ν καὶ

9 ταῖς Εὐμενίδεσι τέλεον, καὶ τõι Διὶ τõι Μιλιχίοι τõι ἐν ΜύσϘο τέλεον τοῖς Τρ-
10 ιτοπατρεῦσι τοῖς μιαροῖς *hόσπερ* τοῖς *hερόεσι, ϝοῖνον hυπολhεί*-
11 ψας δι' ὀρόφο · καὶ τᾶν μοιρᾶν τᾶν ἐνάταν κατακα-
12 ίεν μίαν. θυόντο θῦμα καὶ καταγιζόντο *hοῖς hοσία* · καὶ περιρά-
13 ναντες καταλίναντο · κἔπειτα τοῖς κ<α>θαροῖς τέλεον θυόντο μελίκρατα *hυπο*-
14 λείβον · καὶ τράπεζαν καὶ κλίναν κἐνβαλέτο καθαρὸν *h*ε̑μα καὶ στεφά-
15 νος ἐλαίας καὶ μελίκρατα ἐν καῖναις ποτερίδε[σ]ι καὶ πλάσματα καὶ κρᾶ κἀπ-
16 αρξάμενοι κατακαάντο καὶ καταλινάντο τὰς ποτερίδας ἐνθέντες.
17 θυόντο *hόσπερ* τοῖς θεοῖς τὰ πατρôια · τõι ἐν Εὐθδάμο Μιλιχίοι κριὸν θ[υ]-
18 όντο. ἔστο δὲ καὶ θῦμα πέδα ϝέτος θύεν. τὰ δὲ *hιαρὰ* τὰ δαμόσια ἐξ*h*<α>ιρέτο καὶ τρά[πεζα]-
19 ν προθέμεν καὶ Ϙολέαν καὶ τἀπο τᾶς τραπέζας ἀπάργματα καὶ τὀστέα κα[τα]-
20 κᾶαι · τὰ κρᾶ μὲχφερέτο. καλέτο [*h*]όντινα λε̑ι. ἔστο δὲ καὶ πεδὰ ϝέτ[ος ϝ]-
21 οίϘοι θύεν · σφαζόντο δὲ ΚΑΟΜΤΕΟ[...]Ο ἀγαλμάτον [...] ΔΕΣ[..]..
22 Ο θῦμα *hότι* κα προχορεῖ τὰ πατρô[ια]. ΕΞΑΙ
23 Τ[..].ΙΤΟΙΑΠΤΟΧΟΙ τρίτοι ϝέτ[ει]

Column B
1 ..ἄνθροπος [ ] ..τ.[.(?)ἐλ]αστέρον ἀποκα[θαίρεσθ]-
2 [αι], προειπὸν *hόπο* κα λε̑ι καὶ τô ϝέ[τ]εος *hόπο* κα λε̑ι καὶ [τὸ μενὸς]
3 *hοπείο* κα λε̑ι καὶ <τᾶι> ἀμέραι *hοπείαι* κα λ<ε̑>ι, π{ο}ροειπὸν *hόπυι* κα λε̑ι, καθαιρέσθο, [? *hυ*]-
4 ποδεκόμενος ἀπονίψασθαι δότο κἀκρατίξασθαι καὶ *hάλα* τõι αὐ[τõι]
5 [κ]αὶ θύσας τõι Διὶ χοῖρον ἐξ αὐτô ἴτο καὶ περιστ{ι}ραφέσθο
6 καὶ ποταγορέσθο καὶ σῖτον *hαιρέσθο* καὶ καθευδέτο *hόπε* κ-
7 α λε̑ι. αἴ τίς κα λε̑ι ξενικὸν ε̑̀ πατρôιον, ε̑̀ πακουστὸν ε̑̀ φορατὸν
8 ε̑̀ καὶ χόντινα καθαίρεσθαι, τὸν αὐτὸν τρόπον καθαιρέσθο
9 *hόνπερ hουτορέκτας* ἐπεί κ' ἐλαστέρο ἀποκαθάρεται.
10 *hιαρεῖον* τέλεον ἐπὶ τõι βομôι τõι δαμασίοι θύσας καθαρὸ-
11 ς ἔστο. διορίξας *hαλὶ* καὶ χρυσôι ἀπορανάμενος ἀπίτο.
12 *hόκα* τõι ἐλαστέροι χρέζει θύεν, θύεν *hόσπερ* τοῖς
13 ἀθανάτοισι. σφαζέτο δ' ἐς γᾶν.

12. Herodotus 4.78.3–4.80.5: Scyles and Olbia

The text is based on the Oxford Classical Text ed. C. Hude³ (Oxford 1926).

4.78.3 Βασιλεύων δὲ Σκυθέων ὁ Σκύλης διαίτῃ μὲν οὐδαμῶς
ἠρέσκετο Σκυθικῇ, ἀλλὰ πολλὸν πρὸς τὰ Ἑλληνικὰ μᾶλλον
τετραμμένος ἦν ἀπὸ παιδεύσιος τῆς ἐπεπαίδευτο, ἐποίεέ
τε τοιοῦτο. Εὖτε ἀγάγοι τὴν στρατιὴν τὴν Σκυθέων ἐς τὸ
Βορυσθενεϊτέων ἄστυ (οἱ δὲ Βορυσθενεῖται οὗτοι λέγουσι
σφέας αὐτοὺς εἶναι Μιλησίους), ἐς τούτους ὅκως ἔλθοι ὁ
Σκύλης, τὴν μὲν στρατιὴν καταλίπεσκε ἐν τῷ προαστείῳ,
αὐτὸς δὲ ὅκως ἔλθοι ἐς τὸ τεῖχος καὶ τὰς πύλας ἐγκληί-				4
σειε, τὴν στολὴν ἀποθέμενος τὴν Σκυθικὴν λάβεσκε ἂν
Ἑλληνίδα ἐσθῆτα, ἔχων δ᾽ ἂν ταύτην ἀγόραζε οὔτε
δορυφόρων ἑπομένων οὔτε ἄλλου οὐδενός (τὰς δὲ πύλας
ἐφύλασσον, μή τίς μιν Σκυθέων ἴδοι ἔχοντα ταύτην τὴν
στολήν), καὶ τἆλλα ἐχρᾶτο διαίτῃ Ἑλληνικῇ καὶ θεοῖσι ἱρὰ
ἐποίεε κατὰ νόμους τοὺς Ἑλλήνων. ὅτε δὲ διατρίψειε				5
μῆνα ἢ πλέον τούτου, ἀπαλλάσσετο ἐνδὺς τὴν Σκυθικὴν
στολήν. Ταῦτα ποιέεσκε πολλάκις, καὶ οἰκία τε ἐδείματο
ἐν Βορυσθένεϊ καὶ γυναῖκα ἔγημε ἐς αὐτὰ ἐπιχωρίην.

4.79.1 Ἐπείτε δὲ ἔδεέ οἱ κακῶς γενέσθαι, ἐγένετο ἀπὸ προφάσιος
τοιῆσδε. Ἐπεθύμησε Διονύσῳ Βακχείῳ τελεσθῆναι·
μέλλοντι δέ οἱ ἐς χεῖρας ἄγεσθαι τὴν τελετὴν ἐγένετο
φάσμα μέγιστον. Ἦν οἱ ἐν Βορυσθενεϊτέων τῇ πόλι οἰκίης				2
μεγάλης καὶ πολυτελέος περιβολή, τῆς καὶ ὀλίγῳ τι
πρότερον τούτων μνήμην εἶχον, τὴν πέριξ λευκοῦ λίθου
σφίγγες τε καὶ γρῦπες ἕστασαν· ἐς ταύτην ὁ θεὸς ἐνέσκηψε
βέλος. καὶ ἡ μὲν κατεκάη πᾶσα, Σκύλης δὲ οὐδὲν τούτου
εἵνεκα ἧσσον ἐπετέλεσε τὴν τελετήν. Σκύθαι δὲ τοῦ				3
βακχεύειν πέρι Ἕλλησι ὀνειδίζουσι· οὐ γάρ φασι οἰκὸς
εἶναι θεὸν ἐξευρίσκειν τοῦτον ὅστις μαίνεσθαι ἐνάγει
ἀνθρώπους. Ἐπείτε δὲ ἐτελέσθη τῷ Βακχείῳ ὁ Σκύλης,				4
διεπρήστευσε τῶν τις Βορυσθενεϊτέων πρὸς τοὺς Σκύθας
λέγων· Ἡμῖν γὰρ καταγελᾶτε, ὦ Σκύθαι, ὅτι βακχεύομεν
καὶ ἡμέας ὁ θεὸς λαμβάνει· νῦν οὗτος ὁ δαίμων καὶ τὸν
ὑμέτερον βασιλέα λελάβηκε, καὶ βακχεύει τε καὶ ὑπὸ τοῦ
θεοῦ μαίνεται. Εἰ δέ μοι ἀπιστέετε, ἕπεσθε, καὶ ὑμῖν ἐγὼ

δέξω. Εἴποντο τῶν Σκυθέων οἱ προεστεῶτες, καὶ 5
αὐτοὺς ἀναγαγὼν ὁ Βορυσθενεΐτης λάθρῃ ἐπὶ πύργον
κατεῖσε. Ἐπείτε δὲ παρῆιε σὺν τῷ θιάσῳ ὁ Σκύλης καὶ
εἶδόν μιν βακχεύοντα οἱ Σκύθαι, κάρτα συμφορὴν μεγάλην
ἐποιήσαντο, ἐξελθόντες δὲ ἐσήμαινον πάσῃ τῇ στρατιῇ
τὰ ἴδοιεν.

4.80.1 Ὡς δὲ μετὰ ταῦτα ἐξήλαυνε ὁ Σκύλης ἐς ἤθεα
τὰ ἑωυτοῦ, οἱ Σκύθαι προστησάμενοι τὸν ἀδελφεὸν αὐτοῦ
Ὀκταμασάδην, γεγονότα ἐκ τῆς Τήρεω θυγατρός, ἐπανισ-
τέατο τῷ Σκύλῃ. Ὁ δὲ μαθὼν τὸ γινόμενον ἐπ' ἑωυτῷ καὶ 2
τὴν αἰτίην δι' ἣν ἐποιέετο, καταφεύγει ἐς τὴν Θρηίκην.
Πυθόμενος δὲ ὁ Ὀκταμασάδης ταῦτα ἐστρατεύετο ἐπὶ
τὴν Θρηίκην. Ἐπείτε δὲ ἐπὶ τῷ Ἴστρῳ ἐγένετο, ἠντίασάν
μιν οἱ Θρήικες, μελλόντων δὲ αὐτῶν συνάψειν ἔπεμψε
Σιτάλκης παρὰ τὸν Ὀκταμασάδην λέγων τοιάδε· Τί δεῖ 3
ἡμέας ἀλλήλων πειρηθῆναι; Εἷς μέν μεο τῆς ἀδελφεῆς
παῖς, ἔχεις δέ μεο ἀδελφεόν. Σὺ δή μοι ἀπόδος τοῦτον
καὶ ἐγώ σοι τὸν σὸν Σκύλην παραδίδωμι. Στρατιῇ δὲ μήτε
σὺ κινδυνεύσῃς μήτ' ἐγώ. Ταῦτά οἱ πέμψας ὁ Σιτάλκης
ἐπεκηρυκεύετο· ἦν γὰρ παρὰ τῷ Ὀκταμασάδῃ ἀδελφεὸς 4
Σιτάλκεω πεφευγὼς τοῦτον. Ὁ δὲ Ὀκταμασάδης
καταινέει ταῦτα, ἐκδοὺς δὲ τὸν ἑωυτοῦ μήτρων Σιτάλκῃ
ἔλαβε τὸν ἀδελφεὸν Σκύλην. Καὶ Σιτάλκης μὲν παραλαβὼν 5
τὸν ἀδελφεὸν ἀπήγετο, Σκύλεω δὲ Ὀκταμασάδης αὐτοῦ
ταύτῃ ἀπέταμε τὴν κεφαλήν. Οὕτω μὲν περιστέλλουσι τὰ
σφέτερα νόμαια Σκύθαι, τοῖσι δὲ παρακτωμένοισι ξεινικοὺς
νόμους τοιαῦτα ἐπιτίμια διδοῦσι.

13. Gold Leaves

1. Tablet from Hipponion (=Vibo Valentia), Calabria, South Italy (*c.* 400 BC) (Pug. Car. I A 1, G.-J. 1)
The text is based on that in *Le Lamine d'Oro Orfiche*, G. Pugliese Carratelli (Milan, 2001).

Μναμοσύνας τόδε †εριον† ἐπεὶ ἂμ μέλλησι θανεῖσθαι,
εἰς Ἀΐδαο δόμους εὐηρέας· ἔστ' ἐπὶ δ<ε>ξιὰ κρήνα,
πὰρ δ' αὐτὰν ἑστακυ<ῖ>α λευκὰ κυπάρισ<σ>ος·
ἔνθα κατερχόμεναι ψυχαὶ νεκύων ψύχονται.
ταύτας τᾶ<ς> κράνας μηδὲ σχέδον ἐνγύθεν ἔλθηις.   5
πρόσθεν δὲ εὑρήσεις τᾶς Μναμοσύνας ἀπὸ λίμνας
ψυχρὸν ὕδωρ προρέον· φύλακες δὲ ἐπύπερθεν ἔασι,
τοὶ δέ σε εἰρήσονται ἐν<ὶ> φρασὶ πευκαλίμαισι
ὅττι δὲ ἐξερέεις Ἄϊδος σκότος ὀρφ<ν>ήεντος.
εἶπον· Γῆς παῖ<ς> εἰμὶ καὶ Οὐρανοῦ ἀστερόεντος.   10
δίψαι δ' εἰμ' αὖος καὶ ἀπόλλυμαι· ἀλ<λ>ὰ δότ' ὦ[κα]
ψυχρὸν ὕδωρ πιέναι τῆς Μνημοσύνας ἀπὸ λίμ<ν>ης.
καὶ δή τοι ἐρέουσιν ὑπὸ χθονίωι βασιλῆι,
καὶ δή τοι δώσουσι πιεῖν τᾶς Μναμοσύνας ἀπὸ λίμνας.
καὶ δή καὶ σὺ πιὼν ὁδὸν ἔρχεαι ἄν τε καὶ ἄλλοι   15
μύσται καὶ βάχχοι ἱερὰν στείχουσι κλ<ε>εινοί.

2. Tablet from Thurii, Lucania, South Italy (4th century BC) (Pug. Car. II B 1, F.-J. 3)
The text is based on that in *Le Lamine d'Oro Orfiche*, G. Pugliese Carratelli (Milan, 2001).

ἔρχομαι ἐκ κοθαρῶ<ν>, κοθαρὰ χθονί<ων> βασίλεια,
Εὐκλῆς Εὐβουλεύς τε καὶ ἀθάνατοι θεοὶ ἄλλοι.
καὶ γὰρ ἐγὼν ὑμῶν γένος ὄλβιον εὔχομαι εἶμεν.
ἀλ<λ>ά με Μοῖρ' ἐδάμασε καὶ Ἀσστερβλῆτα κεραυνῶν.
                                        ἀθάνατοι θεοὶ ἄλλοι.   5
κύκλου δ' ἐξέπεταν βαρυπενθέος ἀργαλέοιο,
ἱμερτοῦ δ' ἐπέβαν στεφάνου ποσὶ καρπαλίμοισι·
δεσποίνας δὲ ὑπὸ κόλπον ἔδυν χθονίας βασιλείας.
ἱμερτοῦ δ' ἐπέβαν στεφάνου ποσὶ καρπαλίμοισι.
ὄλβιε καὶ μακαριστέ, θεὸς δ' ἔσηι ἀντὶ βροτοῖο.   10
ἔριφος ἐς γάλ' ἔπετον.

14. The Derveni Papyrus

The text is based on that by R. Janko in *ZPE* 141 (2002) 1–62,

Col. 6
.........εὐ]χαὶ καὶ θυσ[ί]αι μ[ει]λίσσουσι τὰ[ς ψυχάς.
ἐπ[ωιδὴ δ]ὲ μάγων δύν[α]ται δαίμονας ἐμ[ποδὼν
γι[νομένο]υς μεθιστάναι. δαίμονες ἐμπο[δὼν ὄντες εἰσὶ
ψ[υχαὶ τιμω]ροί· τὴν θυσ[ίην] τούτου ἔνεκε[μ] π[οιοῦσ]ι[ν
οἱ μά[γο]ι, ὡσπερεὶ ποινὴν ἀποδιδόντες. τοῖς δὲ   5
ἱεροῖ[ς] ἐπισπένδουσιν ὕ[δω]ρ καὶ γάλα, ἐξ ὧμπερ καὶ τὰς
χοὰς ποιοῦσι. ἀνάριθμα [κα]ὶ πολυόμφαλα τὰ πόπανα
θύουσιν, ὅτι καὶ αἱ ψυχα[ὶ ἀν]άριθμοί εἰσι. μύσται
Εὐμενίσι προθύουσι κ[ατὰ τὰ] αὐτὰ μάγοις· Εὐμενίδες γὰρ
ψυχαί εἰσιν. ὧν ἔνεκ[ν τὸμ μέλλοντ]α θεοῖς θύειν   10
ὀ[ρ]νίθ[ε]ιον πρότερον

Col. 7
ὕ]μνον [ὑγ]ιῆ καὶ θεμ[ι]τὰ λέγο[ντα· ἱερολογεῖ]το γὰρ
τ]ῆι ποήσει, καὶ εἰπεῖν οὐχ οἷόν τ' [ἦν τὴν τῶν ὀ]νομάτων
θέ]σιγ καὶ τ[ὰ] {ῥ}ρηθέντα. ἔστι δὲ ξ[ένη τις ἡ] πόησις
καὶ ἀνθρώ[ποις] αἰνι[γμ]ατώδης. [ὁ δ]ὲ [Ὀρφεὺ]ς αὐτο[ῖς   5
ἄ]πιστ' αἰν[ίγμα] τα οὐκ ἤθελε λέγειν, [ἐν αἰν]ίγμασ[ι]ν δὲ
με]γάλα. ἱερ[ολογ]εῖται μὲν οὖγ καὶ ἀ[πὸ το]ῦ πρώτου
ἀεὶ] μέχρι <τ>οῦ [τελε]υταίου ῥήματος, ὡ[ς δηλοῖ] καὶ ἐν τῶι
εὐθ]ρυλήτω[ι ἔπει. θ]ύρας γὰρ **ἐπιθέσ[θαι** κελ]εύσας τοῖς
ὠσὶ]ν αὐτ[οὺς οὔ τι νομο]θετεῖμ φη[σι τοῖς] πολλοῖς   10
ἀλλὰ διδάσκειν τοὺς τὴ]ν ἀκοὴν [ἀγνεύ]οντας, κατ[ὰ

Col. 13
ὅτι μὲμ πᾶσαν τὴμ πόησιν περὶ τῶμ πραγμάτων   5
αἰνίζεται, κ[α]τ' ἔπος ἕκαστον ἀνάγκη λέγειν.
ἐν τοῖς α[ἰδοίο]ις ὁρῶν τὴγ γένεσιν τοὺς ἀνθρώπου[ς
νομίζον[τας ε]ἶναι τούτωι ἐχρήσατο, ἄνευ δὲ τῶν
αἰδοίων [οὐ γίν]εσθαι, αἰδοίωι εἰκάσας τὸν ἥλιο[ν·
ἄνε[υ γὰρ τοῦ ἡλίου] τὰ ὄντα τοιαῦτα οὐχ οἷόν [τ' ἦν   10
γεν[έσθαι, καὶ γενομ]ένων τῶν ἐόντων [.........
πρ[............]τὸν ἥλιο[μ] πάντα

[τῷ δ' αὖτ' ἐκ Γαίης γένετο Κρόνος, ὃς μέγ' ἔρεξεν]

Col. 14

ἐ]{κ}χθόρηι τὸ{ν} λαμπρότατόν τε [καὶ θ]ερμό[τ]ατον
χωρισθὲν ἀφ' ἑωυτοῦ. τοῦτον οὖν τὸγ **Κρόνον**
γενέσθαι φησὶν ἐκ τοῦ ἡλίου τηι **Γηι**, ὅτι αἰτίαν ἔσχε
διὰ τὸν ἥλιον **κρούεσθαι** πρὸς ἄλληλα.
διὰ τοῦτο λέγει· **ὃς μέγ' ἔρεξεν**. τὸ δ' ἐπὶ τούτωι·   5
Οὐρανὸν Εὐφρονίδην, ὃς πρώτιστος βασίλευσεν
κρυόντα τὸν Νοῦμ πρὸς ἄλληλ[α] **Κρόνον** ὀνομάσας,
μέγα ῥέξαι φησὶ τὸν **Οὐρανόν**· ἀφ[αι]ρεθῆναι γὰρ
τὴμ βασιλείαν αὐτόγ. **Κρόνον** δὲ ὠνόμασεν ἀπὸ τοῦ
ἔ[ρ]γου αὐτὸν καὶ τἄλλα κατὰ [τὸν αὐτὸν λ]όγον.   10
τῶν ἐ]όντων γὰρ ἅπαντ[ω]ν [..........]νων
.....] ὡς ὁρ[ᾶι τὴ]ν φύσιν [...........]ν
......]ς ἀφαιρ[εῖ]σθαι δ' αὑ[τόμ φησι τὴμ βασιλ]είαν
κρυο]μένων τ[ῶ]ν ἐ[ό]ντ[ων

Col. 20

ἀνθρώπω[ν ἐμ] πόλεσιν ἐπιτελέσαντες [τα ἱ]ερὰ εἶδον,
ἔλασσον σφᾶς θαυμάζω μὴ γινώσκειν· οὐ γὰρ οἷόν τε
ἀκοῦσαι ὁμοῦ καὶ μαθεῖν τὰ λεγόμενα. ὅσοι δὲ παρὰ τοῦ
τέξνημ ποιουμένου τὰ ἱερά, οὗτοι ἄξιοι θαυμάζεσθαι
καὶ οἰκτε[ί]ρεσθαι, θαυμάζεσθαι μέν, ὅτι, δοκοῦντες   5
πρότερον ἢ ἐπιτελέσαι εἰδήσειν, ἀπέρχονται ἐπι-
τελέσαντες πρὶν εἰδέναι, οὐδ' ἐπανερόμενοι, ὥσπερ
ὡς εἰδότες τι ὧν εἶδον ἢ ἤκουσαν ἢ ἔμαθον· [οἰ]κτε<ί>ρεσθαι δέ,
ὅτι οὐκ ἀρκεῖ σφιν τὴν δαπάνην προανηλῶσθαι , ἀλλὰ
καὶ τῆς γνώμης στερόμενοι προσαπέρχονται.   10
πρὶμ μὲν τὰ [ἱ]ερὰ ἐπιτελέσαι, ἐλπίζουσιν εἰδήσειν,
ἐπ[ιτελέσ]αντ[ες] δέ, στερηθέντες κα[ὶ τῆ]ς ἐλπί[δος] ἀπέρχονται.

Col. 22

πάν[τ' οὖ]ν ὁμοίω[ς ὠ]νόμασεν ὡς κάλλιστα ἠ[δύ]νατο,
γινώσκων τῶν ἀνθρώπων τὴμ φύσιν, ὅτι οὐ πάντες
ὁμοίαν ἔχουσιν οὐδ' ἐθέλουσιμ πάντες ταὐτά.
κρατιστεύοντες λέγουσι ὅ τι ἂν αὐτῶν ἑκάστωι
ἐπὶ θυμὸν ἔλθηι, ἄπερ ἂν θέλοντες τυγχάνωσι,   5
οὐδαμὰ ταὐτά, ὑπὸ πλεονεξίας, τὰ δὲ καὶ ὑπ' ἀμαθίας.
'Γῆ' δὲ καὶ 'Μήτηρ' καὶ 'Ρέα' καὶ '"Ηρη' ἡ αὐτή. ἐκλήθη δὲ

'Γῆ' μὲν νόμωι, 'Μήτηρ' δ<έ> ὅτι ἐκ ταύτης πάντα γ[ίν]εται,
'Γῆ' καὶ 'Γαῖα' κατὰ [γ]λῶσσαν ἑκάστοις. 'Δημήτηρ' [δὲ
ὠνομάσθη ὥσπερ ἡ 'Γῆ Μήτηρ', ἐξ ἀμφοτέρων ἓ[ν] ὄνομα·   10
τὸ αὐτὸ γὰρ ἦν. – ἔστι δὲ καὶ ἐν τοῖς Ὕμνοις εἰρ[η]μένον·
'Δημήτηρ ['Ρ]έα Γῆ Μήτηρ Ἑστία Δηιώι. καλε[ῖτ]αι γὰρ
καὶ Δηιωι ὅτι ἐδηι[ώθ]η' ἐν τηι μείξει· δηλώσει δὲ [ὅτ]αν
κατὰ τὰ ἔπη γέν[ητα]ι· "Ρέα' δὲ ὅτι πολλὰ καὶ παν[τοῖα
ζωια ἔφυ [ῥαιδίως ......] ἐξ αὐτῆς Ρέα κα[15

15. Curse tablets

Continuous capital letters indicate letters that cannot be divided into
identifiable words.

1. The text is based on Ziebarth (1934) 22 ('Neue Verfluchungstafeln aus
Attika, Boiotien und Euboia', *Sitzungsberichte der preussichen Akademie
der Wissenschaften, Phil.-hist. Klasse*, 33, 1022–1050).

(Side A)
παρατίθομαι Ζο-
  ίδα τὴν Ἐρετρικὴν
  τὴν Καβείρα γυναῖκα
  - [τ]ῆ Γῆ καὶ τῶ Ἑρμῆ, τὰ βρώ-
  ατα αὐτῆς, τὸν ποτᾶ, τὸν ὕ-   5
  πνον αὐτῆς, τὸν γέλωτα,
  τὴν συνουσίην, τὸ κιθ{φε}άρισ[μα]
    αὐτῆς κὴ τὴν πάροδον αὐ-
    [τῆς], τὴν ἡδον<ὴν>, τὸ πυγίον,
    [τὸ] (φρό)νημα, {ν} ὀφθα[λμοὺς]   10
  - - ααπηρη (?) τῆ Γῆ

(Side B)
  καὶ τῶ Ἑρμῆ τὴν | περιπάτη(σι)ν μοχθη | ρ[ὰ]ν, ἔπεα [ἔ]ργα, ῥήματα
  κακὰ | καὶ τὸ

2. The text is based on Wuensch 87 (R. Wuensch, *Defixionum Tabellae Atticae, Inscr. Gr.*, 3.3 (Berlin 1887).

(Side A)

καταδῶ Καλλίαν τὸν κάπηλον τὸν ἐγ γειτόνων καὶ τὴν γυναῖκα αὐτοῦ
Θρᾶιτταν καὶ τὸ καπηλεῖον τὸ φαλακροῦ καὶ τὸ Ἀνθεμίωνος καπηλεῖον
τὸ πλήσιον [...]
καὶ Φίλωνα τὸν κάπηλον· τούτων πάντων καταδῶ ψυχὴν ἐργασίαν
χεῖρας πόδας τὰ καπηλεῖα αὐτῶν.
5 καταδῶ Σωσιμένην τ[ὸν] ἀδελφὸν καὶ Κάρπον τὸν οἰκότην αὐτοῦ τὸν
σινδο[νο]πώλην
καὶ Γλύκανθιν ἣν καλοῦσι Μαλθάκην καὶ Ἀγάθωνα τ[ὸ]ν κάπηλον
τ]ὸν Σωσιμένους οἰκότην· τούτων πάντων καταδῶ ψυχὴν ἐργασία[ν β]ίον
χεῖρας πόδας.
καταδῶ Κίττον τὸν γείτονα τὸν καναβιο(υ)ργὸν καὶ τέχνην τὴν Κίττου καὶ
ἐργασίαν καὶ ψυχὴν καὶ νο(ῦ)ν καὶ γλῶτταν τὴν Κίττου.
καταδῶ Μανίαν τὴν κάπηλιν τὴν ἐπὶ κρήν(η)ι καὶ τὸ καπηλεῖον τὸ
Ἀρίστανδρος Ἐλευσινίου καὶ ἐργασίαν αὐτοῖς καὶ νο(ῦ)ν.
ψυχὴν χεῖρας γλῶτταν πόδας νο(ῦ)ν· τούτους πάντας καταδῶ ἐμ
μνήμασι
               ΑΣΦΑΡΑΓΙΑΙ
10   πρὸς τὸν κάτοχον Ἑρμῆν

(Side B)
τοὺς Ἀριστάνδρου οἰκέτας

3. The text is based on Dubois 37 (L. Dubois, *Inscriptions Grecques Dialectales de Sicile* (Rome 1989)).

(Side A)
  Σελιν<ό>ντιος
  [κ]αὶ hα Σελινο-
  ντίō γλōσα ἀπεσ-
  τραμέν' ἐπ' ἀτ<ε>λείαι τᾶι τε͂νōν ἐγράφō.
  5 Καὶ τōν ξένōν συν-
  δίq̄ōν τὰς γλόσας ἀπε-
  στραμένας ἐπ' ἀτε-
  λείαι τᾶι τε͂νōν
  ἐνγράφō

(Side B)
  Τιμασο͂ι καὶ hα Τιμασō̄ς γλōσα ἀπεστραμέ-
  ναν ἐπ' ἀτελείαι τᾶι τε͂νōν ἐγράφω.
  Τυρρανὰ καὶ hα [Τυρρ]ανᾶς γλōσα [ἀπε]στρ-
  αμέναν ἐπ' ἀτελείαι τ[ᾶι τ]ε͂νōν ἐγ[ράφō] | πάντōν

INDEX

Aeschylus 3, 26–7
Anaxagoras 56, 58, 77, 80
Aphrodite 4, 20, 37, 43
Apollo 1, 5, 12, 19, 20, 29, 30, 32, 61, 64
Ares 61, 64
Aristotle 5, 51–6
Asclepius 62
Athene 2, 5, 8–10, 20, 23
Athlete 22–5, 27–33, 76
Bacchus/Bacchic Cult 69, 70, 71, 72, 73, 74, 75
Carnea 25
Cronus 27, 77, 79, 80, 81
Curse tablets 7, 82–5
Demeter 11, 13, 81–2, 85
Derveni Papyrus 77–82
Dionysus 5, 6, 69, 70, 71, 73, 75, 76
Dreams 18, 21
Empedocles 4, 33–45, 46, 64, 75
Epilepsy 57–64
Epiphany 3–4, 10, 22–3
Erinyes 13, 16, 78
Eumenides 78
Gods (jealousy of) 31
Gold Leaves 73–6
Hades 42, 74, 76, 78
Harpies 41–2
Hecate 5, 18, 19, 20, 22, 61, 82
Hera 10–11, 42
Heracles 30
Heraclitus 39, 78
Hermaphroditus 17, 18, 21
Hermes 20, 82, 83, 84
Herodotus 3, 22–5, 70–3
Hesiod 3, 11–16, 27
Hippocrates 57–64
Homer 1, 2, 8–10
Horkus/Oath 13, 16
Hymn 26–7, 82
Hyperboreans 31–2
Initiation 21, 49–50, 70, 71, 73, 75, 76, 81
Love 33–5, 37, 39, 40, 41, 43, 44, 45, 47

Madness 5, 57–64, 73
Miasma/Pollution 5–6, 11, 15, 21, 22, 39, 57–64, 64–9
Metempsychosis 34, 35, 36
Muses 28, 57
Mysteries/Mystery Cult 16, 21, 46, 49–50, 74
Necessity 35, 39
Nestis/Water 42
Nous/Mind 51, 77, 79, 80
Orphism/Orphics/Orpheus 6–7, 17, 18, 21, 69–82
Pan 3, 22–5
Parmenides 44, 46
Persephone 75
Pheidippides 3, 22–5
Pindar 4, 27–33, 40
Plato 4–5, 45–50, 52, 81
Platonic Forms 45–50
Poseidon 5, 61, 64
Prophet(tess) 57
Pythagoreanism 33–4, 39, 40, 58, 63, 65, 69, 75
Religious advisers/experts 17, 20, 21, 59, 61, 68
Rumour 16
Sabazius 17, 18, 19
Sacred Law 5–6, 64–9
Sacrifice 42
Sappho 4
Scyles 70–3
Soul 39, 40, 48, 55, 75–6, 78, 84
Strife 13, 33–5, 37, 38, 39, 40, 43, 44, 45
Superstition 3, 11–16, 16–22, 64
Thales 43
Theophrastus 3, 16–22
Theoria/Contemplation 51–6
Theoxenia 68
Uranus 27, 79–80, 81
Xenophanes 46
Zeus 3, 5, 9, 11, 12, 26–7, 42, 66, 67, 68, 81